Step by Step Help for
Children
with ADHD

of related interest

ADHD – Living without Brakes
Martin L. Kutscher MD
Illustrated by Douglas Puder, MD
ISBN 978 1 84310 873 3 (hardback)
ISBN 978 1 84905 816 2 (paperback)

The ADHD Handbook
A Guide for Parents and Professionals
Alison Munden and Jon Arcelus
ISBN 978 1 85302 756 7

Kids in the Syndrome Mix of ADHD, LD, Asperger's, Tourette's, Bipolar, and More!
The one stop guide for parents, teachers, and other professionals
Martin L. Kutscher MD
With a contribution from Tony Attwood
With a contribution from Robert R Wolff MD
ISBN 978 1 84310 810 8 (hardback)
ISBN 978 1 84310 811 5 (paperback)

Alphabet Kids – From ADD to Zellweger Syndrome
A guide to Developmental, Neurobiological and Psychological Disorders for Parents and Professionals
Robbie Woliver
ISBN 978 1 84310 880 1 (hardback)
ISBN 978 1 84905 822 3 (paperback)

Step by Step Help for
Children
with ADHD

A Self-Help Manual for Parents

Cathy Laver-Bradbury, Margaret Thompson, Anne Weeks, David Daley and Edmund J. S. Sonuga-Barke

Jessica Kingsley Publishers
London and Philadelphia

First published in 2010
by Jessica Kingsley Publishers
116 Pentonville Road
London N1 9JB, UK
and
400 Market Street, Suite 400
Philadelphia, PA 19106, USA

www.jkp.com

Library of Congress Cataloging in Publication Data
A CIP catalog record for this book is available from the Library of Congress

British Library Cataloguing in Publication Data
A CIP catalogue record for this book is available from the British Library

ISBN 978 1 84905 070 8

Printed and bound in Great Britain by
MPG Books Group, Cornwall

Contents

Acknowledgements

To the many parents who have contributed their ideas of how to manage their child with ADHD and gave us the insight into how to help.

To our colleagues in the local Child and Adolescent Mental Health Services teams and in the universities for their help and support.

Part *1*

What is ADHD and What Can We Do About It?

Chapter **1**

Introduction

What is Childhood ADHD?

All children experience characteristic levels of activity. Some children are very inactive and some are hyperactive. Most doctors and scientists think about activity levels as being on a sliding scale with very inactive people at one end of the scale and very active (hyperactive) people at the other end.

If a child's hyperactivity is causing him difficulty his parents might ask for a professional to meet with them. The child might be in trouble in playgroup or school for not concentrating or sitting down when instructed to, and running around all over the place during quiet activities. The child's parents may also be finding his behaviour very difficult to manage at home.

Note: Although boys and girls can both have ADHD it is more common in boys. For convenience in this guide we refer to the child with ADHD as he – but you need to be aware that the child with ADHD might be a girl. ADHD in girls is often only noticed when they are older, as girls tend to be inattentive rather than overactive.

When an expert in the treatment of hyperactive children, such as a nurse, health visitor or doctor, sees your child he or she may ask very specific questions about his behaviour at playgroup or school and at home, and may also observe him in the clinic setting. He or she may decide your child's symptoms of inattention and over-activity are severe enough for it to be possible that your child has a developmental disorder. That is to say, his symptoms are really a problem for him and he is finding life difficult. The rest of the family might also be finding life with their child difficult, and treatment of some kind might be suggested. The doctor or nurse might call your child's condition 'hyperactivity' or Attention Deficit Hyperactive Disorder (ADHD). ADHD is a syndrome characterised by a collection of symptoms which include hyperactivity, poor attention and impulsivity.

ADHD is not a new disorder. It has been recognized for many years. Recent research has shown, though, how important it is to identify serious ADHD early in life. Early intervention helps children, and helps their families to adapt their parenting approach to the particular characteristics in their child. It is important to start treatment as early as possible to prevent the child's behaviour becoming fixed, which might cause greater problems in the future. Some children who show signs of early ADHD can learn to manage their symptoms with the help of parents and their playgroup or school. It is possible that the symptoms may then stop being a problem for them.

We know that if as parents we can adapt our parenting to our particular child, and help our child to learn to control his behaviour, relationships at home will improve and will be more fun for both parent and child. The child should also do better at school.

We have developed a programme of treatment that is based on what we know about children with ADHD and their families.

The Six-Step Parenting Programme

Children with ADHD need to be parented in a different way from children who are not so active. If you can try these ideas out and practice them you will find that you and your child will get along better.

We will explain to you why children have the kinds of problems associated with ADHD and why different ways of handling the child will work. We have developed a simple treatment programme that you can work through yourself. You can work through the ideas at whatever pace you want. When we use it in clinics with families, they work through it a week at a time, but some families progress more quickly, and others take more time. What is important is to realize that it will not produce instant changes but will over time give you more confidence and provide you with ideas which work for children with ADHD. Practise, more practise, and consistency will produce real detectable changes in your child's behaviour and attitude.

The Six-Step Parenting Programme, originally created by the New Forest Parenting Group, has been the subject of a number of research studies and has been used clinically for a number of years with a diverse range of parents. Whilst many ethnic groups have found some of the advice to be beneficial, in some cultures particular strategies may be difficult to administer. For example, some parents may find using eye contact for positive interactions difficult as their cultural beliefs may mean that a child making eye contact with an adult is not permitted. If you come across a strategy that you find difficult, rather than not use it, try to find a way to adapt it to meet the aim of the six steps within your cultural or personal beliefs. For example, instead of eye contact, touch could be used to signify that the child should listen, and then praise could be given. This would reinforce that the child needs to listen carefully and receive positive feedback, which in turn enables him to listen more and increases his self-esteem. As you will see in Step 1 this is the aim of eye contact in this strategy.

The programme is organized into six steps. We suggest that you work through the material over the next few weeks, reading and concentrating on *one step at a time*. Try out the ideas we have suggested in that step for managing your own child's ADHD symptoms. When you are comfortable with the ideas and confident they are working in practice, *move onto the next step*. As you move on, keep practising the previous steps, if necessary going back to the elements that are not working so well for you and your child.

At each step, the programme will give you something new to work on and suggest you practice it as much as you can. We will also suggest games to play with your child that will help him improve his attention. Most of these games involve using a traditional pack of cards, which is cheap to buy and easy to carry around. We will give you ideas to help your child learn to wait for longer and not be so impatient. We will make practical suggestions that will help your child learn to organize himself better.

The most important aspect of the programme is when we explain to you why a child with ADHD behaves the way he does, so that you can understand that your child's behaviour is the way it is because he has underlying problems, not because he is naughty.

He might, for example, have problems listening, paying attention or waiting his turn.

There will be, of course, times when your child like any other might just be being naughty, so we have to help you learn to identify when that might be the case so you can deal with that too. The fundamental point though is that children who have ADHD have real problems that underlie much of their behaviour and are not, in the main, deliberately being naughty.

We will help you observe your child so that you can work out why he has his own particular problems. This will enable you to tailor the strategies and ideas we present to your own child's behaviour. We hope this means that your child's behaviour improves and, which is very important, that you and your child will get along better. These changes will not take place overnight. It takes time to adapt established behaviours, both for you and your child. Be patient and keep practicing the ideas we give you. Talk to all the other adults who look after your child and try to include them in your plans for change.

Understanding ADHD: What are the symptoms of ADHD?

ADHD is one of the most researched disorders of childhood. The main features of ADHD are:

- a short attention span
- impulsivity (which means that children cannot stop themselves from doing things)
- overactive behaviour.

Parents often find these symptoms very difficult to deal with, and can become very frustrated with their young child. As there is often a family history of ADHD, one or other parent might have symptoms or characteristics of the syndrome too, which can add to the relationship difficulties.

Children with ADHD can have other symptoms as well as the three main elements listed above. Your child may have some or all of them. It might be useful to put a tick against the symptoms or signs of ADHD which your child has, so you can remind yourself that these are part of his ADHD and not just naughty behaviour.

Some children with ADHD may also have poor coordination in *gross motor skills* (for example running and playing games) and / or *fine motor skills* (such as writing or using cutlery). Your child with ADHD may also show the following signs of the disorder:

- a poor short-term memory (remembering things they are asked to do immediately)

- a very active brain, which means that they like to be kept busy

- hating to wait – therefore they will do anything to avoid being bored

- talking and fidgeting when they are supposed to sit quietly

- interrupting when people are talking.

Remember that each child is an individual, though, and therefore the difficulties he presents are unique. Children with ADHD are often very lovable children, but they can be hard work!

Children who have ADHD may also be very emotional children in that they are very sensitive and they can for example believe that other children are making fun of them. They might then hit out, and get into trouble. Parents and teachers can then end up in a negative battle with the child, with everyone getting upset, whereas a more positive strategy takes into account the child's initial sensitivity.

The symptoms of ADHD lead to characteristic behaviours in children. Your child may for example:

- find it hard to concentrate and not be able to continue with activities such as writing or colouring for very long

- move from one activity to another without finishing anything

- rarely play for a long time, and not enjoy playing with toys or games, preferring active games

- often appear not to hear you when you speak to him – if you ask him to do something he will often forget what you have asked him to do

- have a short attention span

- fidget constantly, make noises, talk all the time

- be easily distracted by others

- be reckless, impulsive and prone to accidents.

Research has shown that *children with hyperactivity are four times more likely to have accidents.* It is very important that you help your child to listen when you talk about dangerous situations, for example, crossing busy roads, so that he understands the dangers, and you will need to repeat that advice on a regular basis.

The following common characteristics and problems children may have alongside their ADHD have been reported by parents and researchers:

- difficulties settling for bed and/or getting off to sleep

- waking up through the night or early in the morning

- tending to eat frequent small meals or be a faddy eater, preferring to snack if they are allowed

- social dis-inhibition – a lack of normal caution, speaking to total strangers even though you have warned him not to

- a lack of social skills, being unpopular with other children and having very few, or no, friends

- frequent crying, a poor opinion of himself, and a feeling that no one likes him.

ADHD exists when a child shows a number of the above difficulties both at home and at school or playgroup. It is a complex disorder. As we have said children with ADHD may also have other problems, such as specific learning difficulties, aggression and anxiety or sleeping difficulties.

It is important to see ADHD as a developmental problem rather than an illness. The way your child behaves is not unusual, just unusual for their age. He may be behaving like a much younger child. It is vital that you realize that your child's problems may not go away unless you and he work on changing the behaviour to be more positive. This means him learning how to cope with the problems he has, for example difficulties with attention, overactivity and impulsivity. Some children do not always have all three main symptoms. For example, your child may only have a very poor attention span.

Children with ADHD are more likely to be active when they are young. As they grow older they may grow out of their activity-related problems, but they may continue to have problems with attention and concentration, especially in school. That is why we have written this manual – to help you with your child while he is young, and overactive, and hard work. We also suggest key ideas which will improve your child's attention and concentration and help him thrive in primary school.

Further information about ADHD

There are many books and articles written on ADHD. To understand the condition well, it is advisable that you read more about it. This will give you a greater understanding of your child's difficulties and strengths and how you, as parents, play a vital role in helping your child in the many situations in which they may be having problems, as well as encouraging those areas where they are doing well. A list of recommended useful books and websites is provided at the end of this book on p.156.

It is important that when reading information about ADHD you relate the information to you and your child's particular experience of ADHD. All children and families are different and have different needs. This will enable you to tailor the advice given to your own situation.

Theories about why children have ADHD

There are several theories regarding the causes of ADHD. We describe the main ones in this section.

Genetics

There is research that suggests that the activity level of an individual is genetically determined. It runs in families. It may be that there is another member of your family who is very active too, such as a parent, grandparent, brother, sister, niece or nephew. Your child may have been born with the tendency to be over-active, but rest assured not all such children will go on to have major problems. Some will learn to control their behaviour with the help of their parents and playgroup leaders or school teachers.

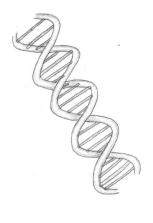

For some children parenting strategies will be sufficient, but for others it may be necessary to go on to consider medication. Generally speaking NICE guidelines in the UK would not recommend medication for children with ADHD under six years of age. This may be different in other countries. Under six years of age in the UK, dexamphetamine is licensed for children from three years of age and some doctors may consider prescribing methylphenidate for children under six years if this seems warranted. Should medication need to be considered, a baseline history should be taken to look for other possible reasons for the child having ADHD and also for possible medical contraindications to starting medication. Baseline monitoring should also be performed.

There is a lot of research into the genes that might be involved in determining whether someone might have an overactive temperament.

The research suggests that the most important genes are those that are involved in producing a chemical called dopamine. Two of the genes that have been found to be implicated most commonly are known as DAT 1 and DRD 4, though others are being discovered all the time. However the genes only work indirectly, and it is a complicated picture since different genes and different parts of the genes will work together. For our purposes the most important point is that there is a direct link between the genes we have and hyperactivity. Not everyone carrying these genes will develop the difficulties associated with full-blown ADHD, however.

As well as genetic reasons for this condition other possible causes for ADHD are illness such as encephalitis, brain injury or lead ingestion. It can be associated with premature birth, cerebral palsy, autism, learning disabilities and chromosome abnormalities. Some children exposed to adverse conditions such as extreme deprivation and abusive situations might go on to have symptoms of ADHD.

The brain in children with ADHD

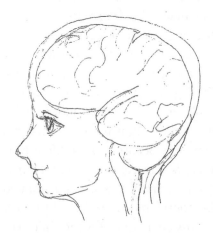

Research suggests that parts of the brain in children with ADHD do not work as well as the brains of children without the disorder, especially areas at the front of the brain. The brain works like an electrical circuit with neurones connecting the brain and parts of the body. For example when a person decides he wants to raise his hand, a signal is sent from the frontal cortex in the brain to the motor cortex, this signal then runs along the neurone to the specific part of the brain that controls the relevant muscles. A signal is sent back down the hand and the hand will be raised. The different neurones involved connect through junctions, called synapses, and chemicals are needed to bridge the 'synaptic gap' between the neurones to pass the message on.

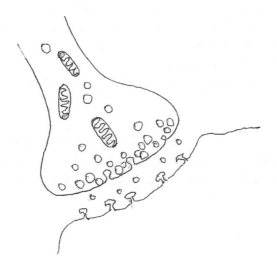

Children with ADHD seem to lack the correct balance of chemicals in these gaps. The chemical that seems to be lacking is dopamine. This means that signals are not carried correctly, and the signals may be carried to the wrong part of the brain (like a train sent off on the wrong track at a junction). This may mean that the child will become impulsive and not be able to stop shouting, for example, as the signal to stop shouting is not working.

Because the front of the brain may not be working as well as it should and may not send messages to the correct part of the brain, other problems may appear as well. These children may have problems with listening. Often they find it difficult to hold eye contact which means it is hard to get their attention. They also find it hard to maintain attention, and therefore become easily distracted. They may flit from game to game, and from task to task. It is hard to get them to sit still and finish a game with you. We call this going off task.

If you ask a child with ADHD to do something, he may forget what you have asked him to do because he has a poor short-term memory. Being organized is also hard, because children with ADHD have problems with planning and carrying out tasks that need to be done in a sequence, like getting up in the morning putting on clothes, brushing teeth and so on. Thus, not only will they get distracted off tasks, but remembering to do it all in the right order is also difficult.

As we have said your child may find it hard to control his impulsive behaviour. So he may get cross easily and hit out. Or he will run off and may be more likely to have accidents. Some children may have problems waiting, and may appear as if they are bored easily. They might find it hard to get motivated to start tasks, to pay attention and to do what you have asked them to do.

Chapter *2*

Parenting a Child with ADHD

We now know a lot, through research and experience sharing, about the kind of parenting which works best for all children, and especially the style of parenting and parenting strategies which work best for children with ADHD. The best results for ADHD children are when a parent can adjust their parenting to the particular child they have, which may not be easy. Some children require one style of parenting and others require other styles.

Parents should communicate and negotiate clearly with their child with ADHD so the child can understand what the parent wants them to do. The child should be able to understand the rules of the house. Rules should be consistent and fair with lots of praise for good behaviour and appropriate sanctions or punishment for behaviour that is not acceptable. The rules, praise and sanctions should be appropriate to the age of the child and be respectful to the child and workable. Parenting can be fun a lot of the time, but doing it right is hard work and requires commitment and the investment of time.

The long-term goal is for your child to learn to control his behaviour with the support of you as his parents and his teachers, and grow up feeling good about himself with the adults he interacts with appreciating his positive points.

What you can do to help your child

We hope that by trying to explain to you why children with too much activity find aspects of life hard, it will be easier for you to understand why they might behave the way they do. This will help you to understand why children who are like this need to be parented differently. We hope that this will make it easier for you to be more positive in your approach to parenting your child with ADHD. We hope you will understand why he behaves this way. This should also make you feel more in control.

For example, when a child with ADHD doesn't listen it is not because he is ignoring you, but because he finds it difficult to listen. We will suggest ways to gain your child's attention in order to begin to try to change his behaviour.

Children with ADHD have real difficulty in organizing their lives so we will suggest strategies that can help.

Behaviour strategies

Behaviour strategies are very helpful for children with ADHD. These are ideas to help parents manage their child's difficult behaviour. As we have said, we know that effective and informed parenting of children with ADHD is very important in preventing them from becoming oppositional and aggressive. We also know that *parenting is extremely hard work* and this is why presenting simple behaviour strategies for parents to follow is usually the first approach.

It may feel to you as parents that you are going over things you may have tried in the past with little success. Understanding the characteristics of ADHD will help you to distinguish those behaviours that the child cannot help, from those which you as parents can help to change.

Changing your parenting approach can be difficult. We have used the ideas we present in this book in our clinic, in groups and individual sessions, and the tried and tested advice in this book has helped many families in several countries. *With a new approach parents often see a big difference in their child's behaviour.*

Below we list some pointers to remember. They will help you to help your child.

- Your child will find it difficult to control his symptoms of ADHD and will find it hard to concentrate and pay attention.

- Nobody is to blame for your child's condition.

- ADHD often runs in families, so you may notice some of the characteristics in family members, or even yourself!

- Adapting your parenting and using the strategies we describe brings about real change in most cases.

It is important to realize that change very rarely occurs overnight. It will usually take a few months to see a significant improvement. It will probably be hard work but worth it in the long run. Changing your parenting approach can be difficult. As far as possible make sure that all the adults who look after your child agree to adopt the same approach to handling his behaviour, and do so in broadly the same way, *as consistency is very important.*

Many families of children with ADHD understandably feel guilty, anxious and angry. Parents may well feel worn out and depressed. Their child may be shunned by friends and neighbours and his behaviour in public can be so embarrassing that the parent avoids social contact outside the home.

There are, of course, different degrees of ADHD and the behaviour of each affected child will be slightly different. The presence of ADHD in a particular child only becomes a problem when his behaviour is unacceptable to others and/or problematic to him. Parents may have managed the pre-school child without noticing a problem until he attends playschool or school, for example. The alarmed parent will then be informed that the playschool or school cannot cope with their child.

ADHD in its extreme form can appear at different stages. Gross motor hyperactivity (like running around) can change to fidgeting and restlessness, for example, as the child has to conform to sitting down for long periods in the school setting. Fidgeting is thus more noticeable in older children.

As well as the main characteristics of ADHD (inattention, over-activity, impulsivity and distractibility) there are usually *associated problems*, as we have seen, which may be the cause of much parental anger and frustration.

To expand on some of what we described in the previous chapter, examples of the associated behaviours exhibited by your child with ADHD may include:

- insatiability, including constant whingeing
- food fads – he tends to 'graze' rather than enjoy proper meals
- difficulty in getting to bed and getting to sleep
- noisiness – he may talk constantly from morning to night
- a lack of understanding of social skills – he tends to invade other people's space, and finds it difficult to be aware of other people's needs
- difficulty in taking turns and sharing
- difficulty making and keeping friends, he may be less likely to be invited to other children's parties, for example
- he may have significant mood swings, with good days and bad days, and possibly, good weeks and bad weeks
- emotional immaturity – he may be at only about two-thirds of the emotional age of his peers
- dislike of change – such as a change of daily routine or a change of carer or teacher
- learning difficulties are frequently present – it is thought that between 40 and 60 per cent of children with ADHD have learning problems, such as difficulty with reading, writing and numerical skills

- problems with language may occur, both with understanding others and sometimes with expressing himself – sometimes these problems can be very subtle and take some effort to remedy.

Children with ADHD have strengths too

There are many positives to having a child with ADHD too, and children with ADHD often have the following strengths of character and show the following positive behaviours:

- they have lots of energy to play and have fun with
- they may be creative and can work out new things quickly
- they may have quick reflexes and do well at sport
- they can think around problems and ways to adapt to new situations when appropriate

27

- they can develop alternative ways of learning
- they can act quickly when you need them to
- they think differently and can be a step ahead of those around them
- when they focus they achieve a lot.

Despite the strengths of a child with ADHD some of the characteristics associated with it can be a real problem that affects children and families. Parents do their best and what you are doing is probably already pretty good, but it may need some fine tuning to make it work for your child with ADHD. What seem to be little changes can make an enormous difference. Increasing your knowledge about ADHD and following the steps outlined in this book will help you to understand and anticipate what is happening. In this book we present tried and tested strategies to help parents. We know from other colleagues' work and research studies that the strategies suggested in this manual will work. The techniques themselves are not particularly difficult, but you may well find them hard at first. We suggest that you have someone, a partner, friend, or parent who may help you and offer some support over the next few weeks whilst you work through the programme.

Personalizing the programme to meet your family's needs

You may need to adapt the programme to suit you and your partners' background. As we said before in some cultures a child gaining eye contact with an adult in a position of authority is not thought to be respectful, so if this is the case, you will need to find others ways of making sure your child is listening to you, especially when you want to praise him. Your religion or culture may not allow the playing of cards (one of the games we suggest to practice working on attention and concentration). If this is so, find other games that do the same task and play them instead.

You may be someone who finds concentration difficult yourself; be fair to yourself and give yourself small 'win-win' (achievable) goals to work on. For example today 'I will work on getting him to give me eye contact to make sure he is listening and I will praise him when he does'. Tomorrow 'I will carry on doing that and work on...'

Children with ADHD who are also temperamentally sensitive

Some children with ADHD are also what is known as 'temperamentally sensitive'. In referring to temperament we mean a child's nature, make-up, the way he responds in different situations. Children's temperaments range from easy at one end, to difficult at the other. Easy children are quick to calm down when upset, are not very fussy, and tend to be fairly happy-go-lucky. Children who are temperamentally sensitive, on the other hand, are not easy to calm down, they may be very fussy, they always want things done a certain way, and they may get upset at the slightest thing.

The characteristics of temperamentally difficult children include:

- he may have been a difficult baby, hard to soothe

- he may not have a regular body rhythm, sleeping poorly

- he gets upset easily and reacts very strongly when upset

- he gets upset about minor things

- he dislikes change and takes time to get used to new situations

- he can be a fussy, difficult feeder

- he can be very demanding

- he may have low self-esteem.

These children tend to get their own way a lot. It may be parents will give in for a quiet life, as whining and crying are exhausting to live with. This could make your relationship with your child unhappy and it may be you will not feel properly in charge. It is likely that your child will not feel very happy either. Children can feel very unsafe about having a lot of control.

As a parent you may feel that nothing you do will be enough, as your child moans at the end of treats, and always wants to stay longer or to have another go. Temperamentally sensitive children are very hard work for parents who inevitably get impatient with them and may become very critical. Below we provide a list of general hints and tips for parents whose children have ADHD and are also temperamentally sensitive.

- It is important for you as a parent to accept the child that you have. The child's temperament is the way it is and if you adjust your parenting style to suit it, life can become much more enjoyable for the whole family.

- Routines and structure are particularly important for sensitive children.

- Children who have sensitive temperaments need some space and peace in their day.

- Clear boundaries are fundamental. Work out which rules are important and which are not. Once you have decided which ones are important, be consistent in expecting those rules to be followed. For example, safety rules are important, but it may not be worth having battles over what your child wears!

- Avoid angry confrontations as much as possible. With ADHD children, defusing a situation early is the best option.

- Improve your child's listening skills. Keep your instructions short and clear. Maintain eye contact by gently holding the child's head if necessary.

- Improve your child's self-esteem by using praise as much as possible when it is appropriate. Warm touches can be helpful here; a stroke or a pat as your child goes past you can be very important. Cuddles and loving touches, even massage, are also helpful to soothe this kind of child. End the day on a positive note.

Understanding that many children with behaviour difficulties associated with ADHD have a very short fuse can help us to avoid some potential pitfalls. It is important to know that the child's outbursts are not deliberate, but part of his inner emotional make-up, which he did not choose.

Professionals working with children with behaviour problems have noticed that sometimes when a child has a fragile temperament this can lead to difficulties with behavioural and social interactions in adulthood. It has also been shown that a difficult temperament at age seven, combined with a lack of consistent family behaviour rules, is strongly associated with significant behaviour problems in the teen years (even worse than normal).

The child with ADHD, as we know, has the triple burdens of impulsivity, hyperactivity and inattention. In addition to this, the child may well be temperamentally fragile. This has important implications for all those who deal with, or live with such children. The way that a parent, teacher or carer handles testing behaviours will depend on how well he or she understands the child's emotional make-up.

Other Ideas to help children with ADHD who lose their temper

If your child with ADHD loses his temper frequently, a *quiet time* is a very effective way of dealing with the difficult behaviour, and encouraging your child to calm down before he actually loses his temper. The technique of quiet time involves taking him away from the situation when he is misbehaving and asking him to sit quietly for a few minutes. (Quiet time and magic carpet techniques are explained in more detail on p.p.116 and 119) It is important that your child is not made to feel that this is a punishment and that he is bad or being rejected, especially as he is likely to have low self-esteem already. Quiet time is about giving children a special space to practice how to calm themselves down and manage their own behaviour. It goes without saying that safety issues must take priority if you think that your child may endanger himself.

Your child should only be left on his own if you feel that you need some time away from your child. This might be because you feel so wound up by his behaviour that you are worried that you might lose your temper, or harm him in some way. All parents can get cross; learning the signs that indicate you are running out of patience is useful, so you can take some time out to calm down. Parents can need different amounts of time to calm down, but the adult brain can take twenty minutes to return to calm following a stressful event. Knowing how long it takes you personally is important, so that you can learn to separate yourself from your child for this period of time whilst finding a safe place for him to go, and/or calling on support whilst you do this.

Much of the advice given to parents about coping with temper tantrums suggests that the child should be gently held until he calms down. We have observed that in some children with ADHD this can be, and usually is, a recipe for disaster (especially those who are temperamentally fragile). So our advice is, find out what works best for your child. If your child with ADHD hates being held, then do not touch, hold, or manhandle him when he is temporarily out of control.

Staying calm

So what do you do? Try to stay calm. Talk calmly to the child as soon as it is possible to do. Say that as soon as he has calmed down, you can be friends; remember to talk about the situation without shouting or blaming. Again, safety issues have to take precedence. It should not be forgotten that some children have incredible strength when very upset and that adults trying to cope with the child can be easily injured if they physically restrain him.

In summary

Children with ADHD need a different kind of parenting.

- It is important to start changes in parenting as early as possible in order to teach the child new skills and to prevent the child's behaviour from causing him ongoing problems.

- It is fundamental that you recognize that this is not your child's fault. He is the way he is, as he was born this way. This will help you begin to accept the child you have.

- Some children who present with early signs of ADHD can be helped to learn to contain their symptoms with the help of parents and the playgroup or school, so that the symptoms may be less of a problem for them.

- We know that if parents can adapt their parenting to their child and help the child to learn to control his behaviour, relationships at home will be better and more fun for parents and children.

- The parent may be parenting well but the parenting will need 'fine tuning' to adapt to the child. This will aid the child's entry to school.

- We believe that if we can help you parent your child differently then you can help him learn to cope better with his problems with ADHD. We will teach you to be your child's trainer.

- You will find it easier to deal with him, and he will get into trouble less. This will help you feel even more skilled in helping him and make your time together more fun and rewarding.

Chapter *3*

An Overview of the Programme

In the Six-Step Parenting Programme outlined in detail in Part II, we suggest strategies to tackle different aspects of your child's problems. Some of things we will introduce to you will include:

- ideas to help you to change your child's behaviour

- ideas to help you improve your child's attention

- ideas to teach him to learn to wait.

By implementing these ideas with your partner and other adults who look after your child, whenever you can, you will help your child to function better in play group, nursery or school. He will be able to sit still and concentrate for longer and he will be able to share and take turns. This in turn will help him to make friends easier.

Remember that there will be good days and some not so good days. This is normal. Sometimes events will go well and sometimes they will not. Just start again the next day if events have not gone well – do not give up. In each step of the programme, we will ask you to review how the previous step has gone, considering what has been successful and what has not. This will help you consider how to change your approach, if necessary.

When you fine-tune how you manage and carry out instructions, do expect that your child may well appear worse for the first few days. This is because he is used to your old ways and change is difficult for him too. The aim is for you, the parents, to understand what is happening – and for us to give you ideas that can help you cope and to improve your child's behaviour.

We know that the ideas we give you might be easy to read, but less easy to put into practice. Yet it does work (eventually!). Most people do not have lessons on child rearing – they have to learn as they go along and often repeat the pattern of their own parents' child-rearing techniques, for better or for worse.

Having ADHD can be an advantage to some people and many people with ADHD are very creative. Some become entrepreneurs, actors, artists, politicians and take up other occupations which require high levels of energy and enthusiasm.

Parents are often worried that 'treating' ADHD will make the child lose their 'spark'. It may be the so-called spark, however, that is causing Mum's heartache. Dad may feel that there is no problem and say, 'he is fine with me'. This can sometimes be explained by the fact that seeing Dad is a comparative rarity and the child may behave better with him. Mothers are normally the main caregivers and they are more 'familiar' to the child. In contrast, Dad may spend only a small part of the day with the child, and the child will view playing and reading and other activities with him as a novelty. The same principle may be seen with grandparents and uncles and aunts, and other adults, so the child behaves better with them than he does with his mother. This may make Mum feel insecure about her parenting skills especially when other adults find it difficult to believe that there is a problem with the child's behaviour.

It is important for the family to understand that the earlier help is given the easier it is to achieve good results. One parent might recognize the difficulties but they might be less obvious to the other parent. School may recognize the difficulties and make it easier for the parents to reach an agreement.

Some parents would prefer a 'wait and see' approach. The fact is, that the sooner help is offered the easier it is to improve behaviour. With every year that goes by without appropriate intervention, it becomes more difficult to bring about change.

The importance of adapting (tailoring) your parenting

As we have said before parenting children with ADHD can be hard work. In this manual we will work with you to try to rethink your parenting toward your child and think of your child in a different way. We hope that you will understand that your child is not deliberately trying to misbehave, or get back at you, and that it is important that you don't take your child's behaviour personally.

As you know it is important that you try to accept the child you have. The child's ADHD and temperament are part of your child's make-up that he was born with. When you adjust your parenting style to your child, life becomes more pleasant for you and your family.

> The most important factor of all, which appears in all six steps: if your child feels valued, worthwhile, approved of and you can spend time with him, he will feel loved and respected.

What affects your parenting?

A recent bereavement, divorce, marital problem, financial problem or mental or physical health problem can make it extremely difficult for a parent to put child management ideas into practice.

Some people expect a sort of magic wand to change their child's behaviour straight away. Unfortunately there isn't one. Parents are the most important people in their child's life and it is you who will be the key person in bringing about changes for the better in your child's behaviour and social development. By adopting the strategies suggested parents can really help their child's behaviour.

You will need to know that parenting a child with significant behaviour problems is emotionally and physically draining. Parents' sense of being made to feel inadequate by this child, and the feeling that they are being blamed for his behaviour may create strong ripple effects impacting on them, the marriage, other siblings, the extended family and the community.

One parent may feel angry if his or her partner denies the problem or withdraws from the situation. One parent may have an easier relationship with the child and this, too, can lead to resentment. If the mum is the main carer, then the husband or partner can feel that he is being excluded by the constant attention given to the misbehaving child, and the same applies to brothers and sisters.

Parents of children with behaviour problems are often (perhaps usually) blamed by lay people and professionals alike. They are given the message that their child's problem could have been solved if only the parent had been 'more this, or more that.' Other parents who have had children without behaviour problems feel certain that the affected parent is inadequate. These lucky parents may be very insensitive to those who have problems. This reinforces the sense of helplessness experienced by parents of a child with difficulties. We know that 'it is very hard work' and that there is no benefit in saying whose fault it is. You are probably doing well under difficult circumstances. *Over the next few weeks we would like you to read the ideas in Part 2, and work on putting these strategies into practice.* We are going to encourage you to find the strength and courage to change the way you are parenting your child so that you can target better his symptoms of ADHD. We are going to encourage you to be his *guide* and *trainer* to guide him to better, more contained, and more useful behaviour.

Remember this will take time, so do not expect an overnight miracle cure. You will see small changes almost immediately as you gain confidence that you can be back in charge of your child (in a positive way).

Parents with ADHD themselves

We have said that the tendency to have ADHD is influenced by genetics. Therefore it may well be that as a parent you have problems associated with the syndrome too. As a child you also may have had problems at home and at school, but may have not known why until we started explaining to you about your child.

If you think you may have ADHD, or some of the signs of it, try to allow for your own ADHD symptoms when parenting. Research has told us that parents with ADHD often find being consistent, organized and calm very difficult. You may need to practise the strategies and your organization skills, and check on your ability to wait, as well as practising listening carefully. Remember that your difficulties can be similar to those that your child is experiencing. Try to identify someone you trust to support you and help you whilst you try to work on your own difficulties.

Parents with ADHD themselves may take longer to work through this manual and its strategies, but remember it is important to keep going even when you have bad days.

The Six Steps – an overview

The six-step programme:

- describes the tasks and skills that we wish you to study and to put into practice – it is a bit like doing course work from home

- explains to you all about ADHD and why children with these problems have the difficulties they do

- discusses with you why we think you should intervene early and try to change things before the child's behaviour becomes more of a problem to himself and others

- discusses what you can do as a parent and how you can change your parenting style to accommodate your child

- encourages you to discuss with your partner or a supportive relative or friend the ideas we have talked about so that you have support at home and so your child has a consistent approach from all that are looking after him

- discusses with you ideas to try out with your child so that you can increase your child's skills

- describes how to be your child's trainer.

As it continues, the programme furthermore:

- describes how to develop your child's ability to do tasks by building on what he can do already and discusses how best to do that so your child can learn independence – this is called *scaffolding*

- asks you to observe how your child does what he is asked to do – we will encourage you to determine what your child can do in order to have the right starting place (this is called *scoping*)

- will encourage you to increase the difficulty of the task as your child masters each stage – for example,

we might ask you to observe how long your child
can concentrate for; we will then ask you to play with
your child for that length of time and encourage him
to concentrate all that time; when you think he can do
that we will ask you to encourage him to concentrate
for one minute longer and so on (this is called *extending*)

- will provide you with ideas on how to improve your
  child's behaviour – for example, when he masters being
  able to come when he is told by cueing him to stop
  what he is doing, we will suggest that the cueing be
  provided less often (*shaping*)

- will give you an explanation about each strategy, and
  why and how to do it and why it is important for you
  to appreciate what is happening – your parenting skills
  may be good; however, if you have a child with ADHD
  your parenting skills may have to be fine-tuned to
  prevent difficulties from occurring later on

- will support you and encourage you to keep working
  on the ideas we have talked about: if you find them
  tough or do not think that they are right for your
  child, think about how you might adjust them for
  your child, talk to your partner or friend and between
  you, you might be able to work out why they are
  not working or what you have to do differently – for
  example, it might be a matter of timing or helping you
  increase your confidence. Practice is important so you
  gain confidence, remember this should be a win-win
  outcome for you, your child and your partner

- will stress the importance of practising at home and
  outside so that your child can use his skills in other
  places, for example sitting still on the bus or at Grandma's
  house, waiting at dinner for his food to be served, or
  waiting his turn to have a biscuit – these are called
  'teachable moments' from which you can generalize what
  you have learned and apply it to other situations.

Part *2*

The Six-Step Programme for Helping Your Child with ADHD

Introduction

Where do we start?

Before you embark on the stages in the six-step programme we
suggest that you make sure you are familiar with the ideas about
ADHD we have outlined in the first part of this book. If you are
unsure of ADHD symptoms then have another look at the open-
ing chapter. It is important that you understand those behaviours
that your child cannot help and those they need help with.

Then you should read the ideas from the first step. Once you
think you are ready, then move onto step two and onwards. In
each step there are tasks that we wish you to study and to put
into practice.

The steps need to be carried out in the order in the book as
the early ones provide the foundations for those that follow. The
first step helps you understand and adjust to your child's ADHD
behaviours. The next step outlines strategies to help children with
ADHD. The third step shows you how to improve your child's
attention through play activities. Communication is fundamental, and the fourth step outlines ways you can improve the ways
you and your child communicate. The fifth step gives practical
guidance on managing your ADHD child outside the home. The
sixth and final step indicates ways forward when your child faces

school or other important life transitions, and re-caps what you have learnt through the programme.

Within the manual you have the opportunity to review the skills and tasks by using diaries and we suggest that you reflect on tasks by talking to your partner or friend as you go along. Some of the things we suggest may seem very repetitive but bear with us as these will help you build on your skills over time and practise will help you to be more confident.

Parents with symptoms of ADHD themselves

We are asking you to be organized, to anticipate and to plan ahead so you can become your child's trainer. This may be difficult for you to do, however it is not impossible. This is a simple six-step programme we have used with many families. You can take as short or as long a time as you need to work through the stages in this manual.

What we have found is that parents who have symptoms of ADHD themselves often need a little longer to first master the tasks for themselves, before they can then help their child. This is fine. Do not lose heart, it is harder for you to do these things, but you will get there in the end.

Work steadily at mastering a task then move on.

Seek someone who can review with you how you are doing.

Sometimes if you have ADHD yourself, you might find it hard to be patient. For example, you have asked your child to do something and he does not do it immediately. Try not to be impulsive and allow yourself to get cross. Try to wait until he has a chance to do it. We think that a parent should try to wait at least *five seconds* to allow the child with ADHD to respond to your request (the *five second rule*), before jumping in and becoming cross.

If your child does not do what you have asked him to do, gently remind him what it is that you want him to do. Remember to make sure you have eye contact when appropriate, and check your child is listening, so that he hears what you have asked him to do.

Remember, if you can, to use choices to encourage your child to do something. If he really is not doing what you have asked him to do then remind him of the house rule and follow the steps you have decided to take when that particular rule is broken.

If you have ADHD yourself you might have to work harder to be consistent and remember what you set as house rules and sanctions. Make sure you do not jump to a more severe sanction than you would have used if you took time to stop and think first.

Reward yourself for each task learnt and completed (for example treat yourself to an evening out with friends or your partner). Remember you are working hard to help yourself and your child… You deserve a reward!

You might have to be even more organized than other parents and get up earlier to have all the children's lunch boxes ready and all your own preparations done, so that all you have to do in the last hour before you set off is sort out your child with ADHD and your other children in the morning before school and work.

In each step we will outline some tasks for you to do and skills for you to learn, so that you and everyone who looks after your child will be able to find new, and more effective ways of dealing with your child's ADHD behaviours.

Step **1**

How does ADHD appear in your child?

Goal for Step 1

The goal for Step 1 is really to understand your child's ADHD behaviours. Each child with ADHD is unique and it is important to recognize the behaviours your child needs help with. If you understand the behaviours that are the result of the ADHD you can start to plan how you might intervene. It is important to have the courage to change long-established behaviours and interactions for the benefit of both you and your child.

It may be necessary to change the way you organize your life to make time to change how you interact with your child. *You are going to become your child's guide and trainer.*

Skills overview for Step 1

The skills you will acquire during this step in the programme are:

1. *how to make eye contact* while giving your child praise – when he is confident in looking at you, then you will learn how to encourage your child to use eye contact

when he is speaking to you and make sure you do the same when you are speaking to him

2. how to recruit your child's attention before giving instructions

3. listening, and helping your child to listen

4. how to start noticing the good things your child does and how to praise him so as to *catch the good*

5. being aware that your child copies you (*mirror image*)

6. begin to notice what your child is able to do

7. practising how you and your child speak to each other showing respect.

Tasks overview for Step 1

The tasks you will carry out later in this step in the programme are as follows:

- read about ADHD again to make sure you understand the difficulties your child may be experiencing

- discuss all the information you have gathered about why a child with ADHD behaves the way he does, with your partner, or relative, or friend so that you can agree on how to change your approach to your child (with their help and support if possible)

- practise all the ideas and keep a diary of how events have been and why some strategies worked and others did not

- make a note of your child's ADHD behaviours that are difficult

- make a note of your child's ADHD behaviours that are good

- write down a list of all the instances of your child's good behaviour (in a diary for good times)!

- Write down all the difficult times you had with your child (in the diary for difficult times).

Initial tasks: preparing yourself

Make sure you understand about ADHD. Try to think about why your child has the problems he does. This will help you to understand why your child behaves this way. It will also help you to find different ways to get him to do what you want. Read Part I again if you need to. Work on having the courage and energy to change things: this will be good for your child and you.

Remember children with ADHD have difficulty listening and paying attention. They also have difficulty waiting and taking turns. They can also be impulsive which is why they interrupt so often. This may happen a lot when you are trying to do something you want, or need to do, like using the telephone.

This will not be easy and you will have to practise using all the ideas in this manual. You may think nothing is changing at first, but keep going, *things will get better.*

Discuss with your partner or a relative or family friend how you are going to work on changing your approach to your child. Enlist their help and support if possible. It is important that all who look after the child work the same way and are consistent

You need to ask yourself if you and your partner disagree on how to discipline your child. If you are miles apart on the issue you will need to try to discuss why you do not agree. Agree if possible that you will work together over the weeks trying out the ideas and talking together to reach a common way forward.

So try to discuss and talk about the contents of the manual at each step and encourage your partner to read and take part in the programme. Listen to yourself when you ask your partner, or a friend, to do something for you. Do you treat your child with the same respect you would use toward your friend or partner? Practise how you want to speak to your child and think through how you are going to speak to them.

Think how you might have to change the way you organize your life to make time to change things with your child. You may need to work on your own organizational skills. We will be asking you to help your child be better organized and think through events before they happen. We will be suggesting to you that you try to anticipate when events and situations might go wrong. This will mean that you will have to be organized as well. You will have to take time to note ways that your child might react so you can work out the pattern of how he behaves.

Use this example notepad as a template for keeping your own notes and records about your child's ADHD behaviours and the things he is good at.

We will ask you to keep a diary as you go along so as you can note down how you are doing. This will allow you to see how you are doing, but also so you can identify all the positive things that your child has done. *Remember you are important as you are going to be your child's Guide and Trainer helping him to develop new ways of behaving.*

NOTEPAD

Keep a note of the ADHD characteristics/behaviours you notice in your child here

I note my child has the following ADHD characteristics/behaviours:

....

....

....

....

....

....

....

My child is good at:

....

....

....

....

....

....

....

Skill 1: Making eye contact

Before giving your child instructions it is very important to get your child's attention. Do not shout messages from room to room. Go to your child.

1. Address him by name.

2. Try to establish eye contact. At first, you should only do this for good or positive behaviour or the child will look away, thinking that he is going to be told off.

This is a very simple skill, but a very important one. Your child needs to be able to look at you without the fear of being told off, so we ask that you *do not make eye contact when you are telling your child off*, but only when you are pleased with him. To encourage eye contact you may need to crouch down and be at your child's eye level. You may need to hold the child's head gently. A tickle under the chin can be a starting point, but both hands may need to be used to get the child to look directly at you. Say, [child's name], 'Look at Mummy/Daddy, please'.

🖈 Tips on eye contact

Most children with ADHD are not good at making eye contact. This can be for a number of reasons, but one major cause is that they have been told off so many times they have learnt to avoid looking you in the eye.

To help your child regain this skill, practise giving him eye contact for positive interactions, when he has done something well. He will soon start to look at you more often, and from then on you can start using eye contact for instructions.

Skill 2: Recruiting your child's attention before giving instructions

Once your child is used to looking at you when you are giving him praise then you can use eye contact when you are giving him instructions.

Your child must be in the same room as you. If he is upstairs on the computer or in another room watching TV, there is no point shouting a message from room to room. You will have to go to him. Gently address your child. Ask him to look at you and give him your message. If you are successful, and your child responds, thank and praise your child for looking at you.

Important note

Many children with ADHD can concentrate for some time on tasks they enjoy (for example watching TV, playing on the computer, using a game boy, and other non-challenging fun activities).

If you were out to dinner and enjoying yourself, and without notice someone came and whisked you away, you would not be very happy. It is the same with children with ADHD. If your child is one minute engrossed in an activity and suddenly to be asked to come to dinner or to stop what he is doing and go shopping, without preparation, it is not surprising that he may have a flare-up.

Because of this difficulty with being interrupted, it is important that you take the steps outlined below.

- *Be in the same room as your child.* Shouting at or speaking to your child when he is in a different part of the house is unworkable. It will appear that he has not heard you if you are not in the same room. This is not deliberate on his part. He can 'switch off' if he is enjoying himself and intrusion into his play or activity will not be noticed. He is still enjoying himself, unaware that you have become annoyed because he has not responded. *You need to be beside him, gain eye contact to make sure he has heard you.*

- *Give him notice in advance.* Give your child this opportunity to adjust – time to switch off, and time to restart. Just like a computer which cannot be instantaneously switched off, because the programme needs to be closed down, which takes a few minutes, your child with ADHD needs time to change from one task to another. Children who have ADHD need to be cued or signalled into a change of task.

  An example of cueing and preparing your child would be to say 'We are going shopping soon, so you will have to stop playing in ten minutes,' then 'Remember we are going shopping. You will have to stop in eight minutes… in five minutes. Three… In two minutes I will come up and then you must stop your game, turn the computer off or pause the game'. Cueing needs to be done gently but firmly with no room for manoeuvre so eventually the child gets the hang of it.

Skill 3: Listening and helping your child to listen

Once you have gained your child's attention, make sure he is listening. Tell him what you want him to do *using short sentences* to keep him listening. Tell him one idea at a time.

If your child wants to tell you something, try to stop what you are doing and turn and face him. Make it clear to him that you are listening. If you have to finish what you are doing, ask

him to wait. Hold his hand if you can so he knows that you are attending to him and you will really stop what you are doing. Then stop the activity you were involved in as soon as possible and turn to face him so you can listen.

It is useful to repeat what he has said to you so he knows you have heard him. Then give an answer. If possible, prolong the conversation, for example, by replying with a question so he has to answer.

Skill 4: Notice the good things your child does and praise him: 'catch the good'

Try to identify positive features in your child.

Children with ADHD are hard work for the carer, and they are often viewed in a negative way. It

is occasionally very difficult for parents to find anything good about their child. This can become a cycle of negativity, and the parents may have forgotten how to praise their child. They may find that they cannot bring themselves to give praise because they cannot forget the naughty things their child has done at another time. It is important to treat your child as you find him and not to be affected by your residual feelings to do with incidents that are over and done with.

Try to work towards viewing your child more positively instead of looking at the more negative aspects. Your child and you may well be out of harmony and this may have made discipline problems get bigger. This may cause over-reactions from both of you to every issue.

Start with small nuggets of praise. When your child does something good say 'well done' and at the same time emphasize what he has done so he knows what it is your are praising. For example say 'Well done Johnny for tidying your toys up I'm really pleased with you'. This is known as *capturing the moment of good behaviour.* This is especially important for a child with ADHD as he may well have done something good, but then quickly gone on to do something wrong.

For example, it is important that a child knows he is being praised for stopping jumping on the chair, not for doing what he did next which was to snatch his brother's toy car.

Later, aim to use praise to encourage longer periods of acceptable behaviour, too, for example 'When you did that [say what it was], it made me so proud [or pleased, happy, delighted, glad etc.]'.

Words such as 'good' and 'bad' need to be broadened because they are words that we tend to use excessively and because the child may not really have an understanding of what good and bad really mean. That is why you need to say to your child precisely what he did that you disliked or approved of.

You can also praise using body language, a smile, thumbs up, wink and so forth. Later written praise can be given if the child understands, such as kisses (xxxx) on notes you write him.

Skill 5: Be aware: Mirror image

When you are praising, observe your body language. For example when you say well done, do you genuinely mean it, or is your body language wrong? Are you smiling, or not, are you frowning, looking angry? It is hard if you are depressed or unhappy but it is worth highlighting that if you are going to praise your child, then *try to smile*, even if you do not feel like it. If your child hears you saying 'well done', but you are frowning or looking cross, the child will get a mixed message and not really know what you are trying to say. Remember most children (like adults) look at the eyes for clues to emotion and the meaning of messages.

Skill 6: Begin to notice what your child is able to do

Start noticing the extent of your child's abilities so you know what you need to work on to change things. For example your child might be able to concentrate for only three minutes on a game or colouring.

Even though you may think that he should be able to dress himself, when you watch him you may realize that he is so easily distracted that you may need to be with him to encourage him to stay on task with gentle reminders. Noticing what your child can do or has difficulty with is called *scoping*.

It is important in this step to note how long your child can wait for, how long he can concentrate for and to generally keep note of what your child can do. *Scoping makes you aware of where he is experiencing difficulties and what he will need you to help him with.*

Skill 7: Remember to speak with respect to your child

Talking in a calm factual way helps your child to learn to speak to you with respect. You should speak to your child as you would a friend or colleague so you both learn to interact more positively.

Tasks for Step 1 you need to carry out now

Make sure you understand as much as you can about ADHD and how this affects your child by reading more about it, for instance why not consider getting hold of some of the resources we list on p. 161.

Keep two weekly diaries one for positives and one for difficult situations

We ask that you keep two diaries: one to write down any difficult situations that have arisen and the other to write down all the things that have gone well. The diaries can be used to see how practising the ideas has gone, and they provide you with the opportunity to review why you think some things have worked and others have not. We have included two diary pages for you to complete, one for good and one for difficult times, at the end of each step in the manual. You could make your own diaries if you prefer.

Remember to share together with your partner the things you have noticed your child has difficulty with, and the things he is good at. It is important that you work together and support each other in helping your child. If you can agree on how to manage your child it provides him with consistency and he knows both parents understand his difficulties and are trying to help him.

Recap and review

What we have covered in Step 1 is reviewed below. Don't just skip this section. Use it as a checklist when you look back at your diaries for the week. How well have you done in achieving the goal? Which skills did you find easy to use and which more difficult? Have you carried out all the tasks?

Goal for Step 1

The goal for Step 1 was to really understand your child's ADHD behaviours. Each child with ADHD is unique and it is important to recognize behaviours your child needs help with. If you now understand the behaviours that are caused because of the ADHD you will be able to start to plan how you might intervene. It is important to have the courage to change things for the benefit of both you and your child.

It may be necessary to change the way you organize your life to make time to change the ways you interact with your child. It is worth repeating – you are on the way to becoming your child's guide and trainer.

Skills summary for Step 1

The skills you acquired in this step were:

1. Making eye contact while giving your child praise. When he becomes confident in looking at you, then you encourage him to use eye contact when he is speaking to you too.

2. Learning how to recruit your child's attention before giving him instructions.

3. Considering your own listening skills and helping your child to listen.

4. Noticing the good things your child does and to praise him so as to 'catch the good'.

5. Becoming aware that your child copies you (mirror image).

6. Practising speaking to each other showing respect.

The tasks for Step 1 reviewed

- Have you to read about ADHD again to make sure you understand the difficulties your child may be experiencing?

- Have you discussed all the information you have gathered about why a child with ADHD behaves the way he does with your partner or relative or friend so that you can agree on how to work on changing your approach to your child?

- Have you practised all the ideas and written in the diary how the week has been and why some elements in this step worked and others did not?

- Have you made a note of your child's ADHD behaviours that are difficult?

- Have you made a note of your child's ADHD behaviours that are good?

- Have you written down all the good things your child did (in the diary for good times)?

- Have you written down all the difficult times you had with your child (in the diary for difficult times)?

If you think you understand how your child's ADHD is affecting him and have practised the skills and completed the tasks you can now move on to Step 2. Remember that at any time you can repeat a step if you need to, and each parent can move through the steps at his or her own pace.

Diary for good days

Date . . . .

Time . . . .

What made it good? . . . .

. . . .

. . . .

. . . .

What did you do? . . . .

. . . .

. . . .

. . . .

Did it help? . . . .

. . . .

. . . .

. . . .

. . . .

How do you feel now? . . . .

. . . .

. . . .

. . . .

Diary for difficult days

Date . . . .

Time . . . .

Trigger . . . .
. . . .

What Happened? . . . .
. . . .

What did you do? . . . .
. . . .
. . . .

Did it help? . . . .
. . . .
. . . .

How do you feel now? . . . .
. . . .

Would you do anything different? . . . .
. . . .
. . . .

Step **2**

Strategies to Help
Children with ADHD

Goal for Step 2

The goal for Step 2 is to build on Step 1 by understanding your child's ADHD you can start to apply the skills we outline below based on your assessment of your child's difficulties. In this step the goal is tailoring the strategies in the manual to your child's difficulties in your role as his trainer.

Skills overview for Step 2

The skills you will acquire during this step in the programme are:

1. how to start using *scaffolding* what your child can do

2. how to identify and use *teachable moments*

3. *earshotting*

4. how to adopt a *consistent routine*

5. how to set clear *behaviour boundaries* and *house rules*

6. how to use *countdowns* and *delay fading*

7. learning to give *clear messages* (remember eye contact)

8. using short sentences

9. using choices

10. avoiding confrontations and arguments

11. keeping calm

12. calming your child.

Remember when changing your approach

First, it is important to realize that change rarely happens over-night and that it may take a few months to see a significant improvement. We know the skills you adopt will help you to teach your child and improve his skills over time. However, we would expect that you will see change in some things immediately.

Try to ensure that all the adults who look after your child agree how to handle his behaviour and do so in broadly the same way. Consistency is very important. As we have already said it is important for parents to try to accept the child they have. The child's temperament is the way it is, and by adjusting your parenting style, life can become more pleasant for the whole family.

Later in this chapter are some diary pages to help you assess your child's abilities. You can use these to help you see your child's progress over time.

Some parents find some skills easier to adopt than others. If you are having difficulties using a particular skill ask your partner if he or she is experiencing the same difficulty. If they are you may be able to think of an alternative together which achieves the same goal. *Don't give up, keep trying.* Sometimes it just needs a bit more practice.

Tasks overview for Step 2

The tasks you will carry out later in this step in the programme are as follows:

- continue to work together with your partner

- remember to keep trying skills out over and over again

- learn to manage behaviour while being realistic about what you can achieve

- remember to practise the skills from Step 1, including eye contact, listening and praise

- start playing games to help improve your child's attention

- play together for at least ten minutes a day

- keep a diary for difficult times

- keep a diary for good times.

Thinking through how the first step has gone

Have you managed to identify positive things that your child has done and praised him, making sure it was clear what you were praising him for? Looking at the diaries from Step 1 you should have some examples of what went well and what helped to ensure things went well.

Have you made the connection between your child's behaviour and the reasons why he might behave the way he does? Remember, due to his ADHD your child may find it hard to listen and to remember what you have asked him to do. He may start off doing things and then get distracted (very annoying to a parent but understandable for a child who finds it hard to stay on task). We will encourage you to help your child finish something he has started.

Spend time looking at your diaries of both the difficult and the good. See if you can identify triggers for difficult situations.

If you can see a pattern it helps you to avoid repeating difficult events in the future.

As your child's parent, you are his guide and trainer. We can give you advice and ideas but you will have to carry them out yourself (we hope with the support of a partner or friend).

Skill 1: Scaffolding

Every child has different skills and it would be helpful to take some time to map out what your child can do. As mentioned in the last chapter we call this scoping. Scoping is when you as a parent assess the range of your child's abilities at this moment in time. The *planner* at the end of this week's notes is for you to use to map out what your child can do. Scoping of this sort is the first stage of what is called scaffolding.

For example how long can your child concentrate for? We can build on getting him to concentrate for longer. How good is he at listening or coming when you ask him to? Once you have built up an idea of how long he can wait or how well he listens, you can build on his abilities and help him to extend his skills.

Knowing how your child is functioning can help you pick the right level of toys or games for him to play with, and enables you to judge when to challenge your child to improve his development. This gradually builds up the set of skills which your child can do easily. You then *extend* his skills with tasks that might take a little longer without the child getting cross and losing interest, or as important, losing his self-esteem.

The stages of scaffolding are:

- *scoping*: watching your child to see what he is able to do

- *mapping his zone of proximal development*: identifying exactly what your child is able to do on his own and how much he could be encouraged to do with you providing the scaffold

- *extending*: helping your child to work on a task a little bit harder than he can do on his own

- *consolidating*: practising the skills to ensure your child has learned them properly.

We have added a 'Review Sheet' for you to complete yourself (on p. 83) at the end of this step. It will help you reflect on your child's ability. This sheet will be repeated in Step 6 to enable you to keep a check on your child's progress, and you can design your own too.

Skill 2: Identifying and using teachable moments

Once you suggest a new idea to your child, practise it in different settings. We call that *using the teachable moment*. This means grabbing any opportunity to practise a skill. We are going to suggest games to play with your child that will improve his memory and his attention. You can work on this when you go out on a walk, in the car or in the supermarket, café or pub, or at a friend's house or at Granny's.

Skill 3: Earshotting

Praising in 'ear shot' works well. For example, when your child can hear you, Mum says to Dad or grandparents [child's name] did...... [state what] today and I was so proud of him because he was gentle, (considerate, kind, affectionate etc.) with [whoever]. Isn't that wonderful.' You can do this on the phone too when your child is in ear shot.

Skill 4: How to adopt a consistent routine

Provide routine. A child, particularly a child with ADHD, needs to know in advance what is going to happen each day. If the routine changes, let him know. Plan ahead. Plan around tiredness, sleep, hunger and expected mood changes.

Try not to go shopping when the child is hungry or tired, it will only cause difficulties.

Children with ADHD do not like any change of routine. Plan ahead for the day, give advanced warnings, discuss what you are going to do, and reassure your child that he will like it. On the other hand *do not tell your child about events that are happening many weeks in advance,* otherwise you will be badgered about 'When? What? Where'?

Here's an example: 'Tomorrow we are going on a trip, by car, with Daddy. We are going to stop at [ ] to have a lovely picnic together. Then we will drive a little bit more and then we will arrive at Grandma's. At Grandma's we will have tea and then you can play with Grandma and Grandpa. Then we will drive back home in the car.'

Scope what your child is capable of coping with. If that would be too much information give him as much advance knowledge as he can cope with, and then give out more as you go along.

Keep a diary and note any difficulties carrying out the above tasks. Talk them over with your partner. It is useful to keep a diary so you can look back and compare notes week by week.

Below we give an example of a plan (again, share only as much as your child can cope with at a time).

PLANNERS USING PICTURES

For some children drawing pictures of the plan of the day works well especially for children who do not yet have good language skills. You can cut out pictures from magazines.

A normal day plan might have less on it, but you could have pictures you use every day e.g. for breakfast, school etc. This is especially helpful for children with poor language and those who are unable to read yet.

If your child has problems with unstructured time it is worth putting in his planner 'free time' and then help him to structure his own time using his own ideas.

Saturday's Plan

8.00 am	Get out of bed
8.15 am	Wash face and clean teeth and get dressed
8.30 am	Eat breakfast
9.00 am	Pack your toys to take to Granny's (remember books and toys)
10.00 am	Arrive at granny's have a drink and PLAY
12.00 pm	Lunch with Granny and Grandpa
1.00 pm	Go for a walk
2.30 pm	Have a drink and snack with granny play games
4.00 pm	Go home in the car
5.00 pm	Play with Dad or watch TV before tea
6.00 pm	Eat tea
7.00 pm	Have a bath, clean teeth, and go to toilet
7.30 pm	Bedtime and story
7.45 pm	Lights out, time to sleep

Skill 5: Giving clear behaviour boundaries and house rules

Having boundaries means setting limits and rules. Children need boundaries otherwise they do not feel safe. Sometimes boundaries or limits are not clear. We tend to forget to say, 'this is what I/we expect of you.' In the case of a strong willed child we tend to

- give-in to the child

- be too busy or tired to get him to obey requests

- make excuses, such as, 'it's a stage he is going through'.

Children often do not actually know if their behaviour is acceptable or not, unless you tell them.

Children will test their parents daily. They want to see if you have moved the goal posts and to see if they can really trust you. If you keep moving the limits or goal posts or don't stick to the rules you have made, your child may become anxious and frightened, and his behaviour frequently reflects this. This is even more likely to happen to children with ADHD. This is because they tend to make lots of demands each day. So as their parents you need to have even more understanding, insight, energy, patience, maturity and creativity than other parents.

We are not talking here about 'obey or else' situations which will cause the child to behave out of fear rather than respect. You need to be warm, gentle and clear to enable your child to respect you. This also helps the child to respect authority from other people such as playgroup leaders and school teachers. Again, setting an example in the family is important, for example, if parents are rude with friends or relatives, this is what the child learns to imitate ('another example of *mirror image*).

House rules

This week, decide on a rule you are going to work on and praise the child when he follows that rule. Start with something simple like reminding him that he has to come when called, for example when it is lunch time soon, and then praise your child when he comes when asked to do so.

You want to start helping him to understand that by doing what he is asked to do you will praise him and be pleased with him.

Discuss with your child which rules are important, and which are not. Decide which ones you are going to work on first. Pick only one or two and not more than three to focus on at a time. Write them down. Make sure everyone in the house agrees what they are going to be, and sticks to them. *Remember to make sure that your child is praised for keeping the rules.* Work out a system for accompanying praise with a concrete reward, for example an extra story, more time to watch a favourite DVD.

Remember though that first of all you have to get your child's attention. Make sure he has listened and understood what you have asked him to do. Always remember to *catch the good:* when your child has done something good *praise* him. If you think your child will understand you can start working out rewards for good behaviour, once you have established a pattern of praising his good behaviour.

 Tip on the importance of praise

Praise your child whenever you can.

Look pleased to see him when you pick him up from school, he may have had a hard day.

Remember children often act out what they see! You smile, they smile!

Skill 6: Using countdowns and delay fading

Reminders, clocks and timers

Reminders such as clocks, timers and warnings are ways of letting your child know that something is going to happen very soon (for example bedtime, or going to the shops). All children benefit from having reminders as they are a clue to jog their memory. Reminders are also less likely to prompt a refusal or a power struggle than an outright command. Children with ADHD have much more difficulty managing time than those without ADHD. Therefore it is very important that these children practice time management. These are techniques that have to be learnt.

Use visual clues, for recognition of time with your child. For example, show, explain and say 'When the big hand is on... [Show child] we are going to... We are not expecting you to teach a young child how to tell the time but even small children can manage to see the big hand on a clock has moved by five minutes.

Buzzers, timers (like an egg timer) and alarms are also useful aids to remind the child about time.

📌 Tips on the use of timers

Timers can be used in all sorts of ways:

- to help remind the child of a change in situation ('When the timer goes off we will leave Granny's to go home')
- to start a new task ('It's now time to clean your teeth')
- to have 'calm down' time (either for the child or yourself)
- to signal the start and end of a period of 'fun time'.

Countdowns and warnings

Countdowns, when you tell your child 'we are leaving in ten minutes; we are leaving in five minutes and so on', give the child time to prepare to finish his task, compared to a sudden 'we are going now' without a warning which would inevitably cause a scene. Remember to keep warning the child with time cues. When it comes to the last two minutes, 'I will be up in two minutes and you will need to stop playing, save your game'. Make sure your child knows that he will have to stop and do not allow him to try to prolong the game. He will gradually get the message that stopping time is stopping time.

Teach your child to cope with waiting for something he wants. We call this *delay fading*. For example your child wants a biscuit. Lunch is going to be in ten minutes. You answer: 'lunch is in ten minutes – you can have a biscuit after lunch' (*note that you avoid the word no*). 'Then say, 'let's see what you can do to make waiting for

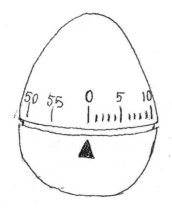 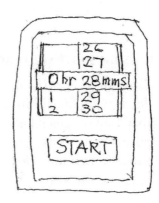

lunch easier. Do you want to do a drawing or some colouring or build me a Lego car?'

Of course what is really important is that you also pay attention to time. If you say to your child that you will be ready in a minute, is your minute really a minute or actually five or ten minutes? Think about what message you want to give your child about keeping to time.

Always keep your warnings and countdowns clear and brief.

Skill 7: Giving clear messages (remember to use eye contact)

There is no point in asking your child to do things which are too complicated. Keep your sentences and commands short. *Keep it simple* (KIS). One idea per sentence. Do not give the child more than one command at a time until you are sure he can manage to remember more than one *(an example of scoping)*.

When you want your child to do something, first make sure you have eye contact, and your child is listening. Speak in a clear voice indicating that you expect him to do what you ask him to do. This does not mean an angry voice, just a voice that is firm (like when a bus driver says 'move along the bus,' or 'take your seats'). When you want something done, give commands not questions. If you say 'Will you tidy up now?' your child can always answer 'no'. Instead say, 'Tidy up now please'.

Skill 8: Using short sentences

Remember *keep it simple* (KIS) – use short sentences.

Children with ADHD have poor short-term memories. This means they cannot remember long or detailed tasks.

Practice a one sentence rule, with sentences of no more than three to four words, and possibly ask your child to repeat it back to you when you've said it. This way it helps him to remember.

Skill 9: Using choices

When you do give choices, give only two choices. This will make it easier for your child to make up his mind, and reduces the opportunity for him to say no. *Always make sure that the child has heard the message and understands.* Ask the child to repeat the message back to you.

For example, 'Do you want cheese or ham for lunch?' If your child takes a long time to make up his mind, or he is unsure say, 'Are you choosing or shall I choose for you?'

You should be aware that in a group situation if all the other children choose something and your child opts for something different, your child may not later be happy with his choice. If in doubt say, 'Everyone else is having a.... do you want the same or not?'

📌 Tip on giving two choices

Give limited choices for example 'Do you want a tuna or an egg sandwich?' Remember the child's short-term memory problem and impulsivity, so ask him to repeat what it was he wanted.

Another example is 'Do you want me to help you with your coat or are your going to do it yourself?' This strategy should lessen the chance of your child replying 'No'.

Skill 10: Avoiding confrontations and arguments

Young children often say 'No'. This is part of normal development, because they are learning to develop a sense of self. They try to discover what power they have. However they need to learn how to give and take. Try to remember that this challenging behaviour is normal and that you must not feel threatened by it. You, the parent must try to recognize that after a while the whole argument and confrontation becomes a game. As parents you need to recognize this quickly and ask yourselves what is happening, so you can avoid rows. You know that arguments won't achieve the outcome that you want to.

It takes two to argue. You as the parent have to be adult about the situation and say something like, 'I have said (avoiding the word *no*) *yes* you can have a biscuit after your lunch. I am not talking about it now.' You should then walk away. Don't keep the argument going even if your child tries to. Remember when you are out and about with your child you can practice skills and techniques for example, getting his attention, getting him to listen to you as well as you listening to him. This programme will help you to help your child to learn to wait, and to help him practice and improve his memory with games. But you can do that anywhere. If you go shopping, ask your child to remember to tell you to get something you need like milk, and praise him when he reminds you.

You can gradually build up the number of things your child has to remember. These are the teachable moments we talked about before. We want to encourage you to use them whenever you can, generalizing learning to a different environment.

The combination of a difficult child and a parent with a short fuse can often mean that major conflicts happen. Many parents with a hyperactive child feel they have tried everything and nothing works. In desperation they use shouting type behaviour themselves.

Skill 11: Keeping calm

One of the key skills that parents have to learn is *keeping calm*. If you shout, your child also shouts when he is angry and *mirrors your behaviour*. Children copy what they see going on around them and if Mum and Dad shout at each other when cross, your child will do the same when he is frustrated or angry.

Keeping calm is something you have to learn and work at. So practice. Practice and discuss with your partner or friend alternatives to shouting.

One of the techniques that we have found works well is to practice bringing down an *imaginary perspex screen* in front of you (like the shields that police use when they go into riots). You can give yourself a cue to 'bring it down' by rubbing your ear for example. When you imagine that it is in place then you say to yourself that no negative emotions can reach you. Practice doing this when you feel you are getting angry. Take a deep breath. If you practice it so that immediately you feel you are getting angry the screen comes down you can stay calm behind it and deal with your small child more calmly because his crossness 'will not reach you', but you can still 'see out'.

Most parents want to explain to their child why it is so important that he does what he has been been asked to. This is fine, but not at the time of crisis.

1.   First remove the danger.

2. Let everybody calm down.

3. Only when everyone is calm explain the reasons.

Keep the explanation short and concise, remember their short term memory problems. Do not do the explaining hours later otherwise the child will have forgotten about the incident.

If the child is in a *dangerous position, always try and stay calm.* Many children have fallen and had severe accidents when someone has screamed and shouted at them. This is difficult because it tends to go against our instincts. Practicing calm instructions in a safe environment helps one not to shout in difficult circumstances.

Try to stay calm, try to soften your voice. The child will have to come down to your emotional level to receive your attention.

Here's an example: If you are returning something to a shop, you may be going in ready to have a 'verbal fight' about it. The shopkeeper says calmly, 'Yes, Madam. I will refund your money.' This defuses the situation. Try the same technique with your child. Stay calm, the situation could be easily defused if you do not respond by shouting. So *calmly does it.* Give your message in a calm voice and use a respectful tone.

Parents may not like their child having the last word, but unless this is a big problem (it is part of normal development, part of developing independence) learn to walk away and not let it irritate you. Remind yourself it takes two to have an argument; one person has to be adult about it and walk away.

Write down what really irritates you, and which behaviours can be ignored. For example, whining can be ignored (although it can be very annoying) but some behaviours cannot be ignored such as hitting, biting and kicking.

Skill 12: Calming your child

If you have an argument with your child, he may have a temper tantrum because he is frustrated, emotionally overloaded, tired, bored, hungry or over-stimulated. Tantrums will be discussed in more detail later.

You cannot ignore the tantrum, because through it your child is saying, 'Do something! I am out of control.' By offering to help the child out of a difficult situation you can help to build authority, trust and convey that you are in charge of the situation.

Say calmly, 'Calm down. When you are calm we can be friends' or 'then we can have a cuddle'. Try to say this only once.

Do not make the message too long. Do not ask why they did what they did and so on. Ask questions like this only when things are calm. During a tantrum:

- your child is not listening
- your child does not know rational answers anyway
- you are wasting your breath and energy.

📌 Tips on keeping you and your child calm

- Make sure consequences are short and realistic. If possible negotiate these with the child.
- It is better to explain that a rule has been broken and why a consequence has been enforced than to shout.
- Keeping calm is one of the most difficult things to do, but probably the most important.
- Separate the child's behaviour from the child for instance say, 'I love you, but I don't like it when you do…'
- Don't threaten unless you mean to carry through your threat.
- Don't use sarcasm: children with ADHD don't understand it.

Task: using play to help your child's attention and concentration
Games to help improve memory

Children with ADHD often have problems with attention, concentration, memory, taking turns and losing at games. As a result of this they often find playing very difficult. In the first instance we want the play to be aimed towards your child succeeding, so it is important to prepare before you start to play. Your aim is to help them win by using smaller numbers of cards which you know contain pairs. Over time you should make this more difficult but at first you just want them to enjoy the game and want to play it more.

These games will help your child's working memory. Try to play these games with your child for at least ten minutes a day.

SNAP

This game is useful for teaching your child to (i) attend (ii) concentrate (iii) improve his memory (iv) take turns and (v) learn to cope with losing.

The beauty of this game is that as it is a very quick game to play and finish the child knows that a new game will follow in close succession.

Divide up a pack of cards, shuffle them, so that the cards go out of order, then sit facing each other. One by one take turns to turn over the cards placing them in the middle of the table. The first one to spot a pair (a similar card turned up by their partner to the one they have turned up) and shout out 'snap' gets the whole pack in the middle. The game continues until one player has collected the whole pack. Then the next game begins according to the same rules. It is useful to put a time limit on the length of play.

You might want to start playing with only a few cards to begin with. If that is the case, make sure you have enough matching pairs in the ones you do play with otherwise you and your child will get bored quickly!

Make sure everyone who is playing, is playing to the same rules.

You could keep a running tally or work out the winner each time you play.

It does not matter if your child looks at his card at first before laying it down, it is more important for him to feel confident in matching the cards. It is important to help your child win some of the time. You can make it more difficult later on.

✒ Tip: the importance of playing together

Children with ADHD have problems concentrating. They often miss out on learning through play.

Play games with your child as often as possible (for at least ten minutes each day). Don't make these competitive games, but just have a fun time. They can be indoor or outdoor games, whichever you enjoy together.

By doing this you will also help your child learn to play with his friends.

The tasks for Step 2

The tasks in this step have been embedded in the skills. You also need to remember to work together with your partner, family or friends to provide consistency of approach for your child. If possible use the skills from Steps 1 and 2 both at home and outside the home, though it is important to practice them as much as possible at home first to give you confidence in using them.

Discuss with your partner whether he or she could play snap to improve your child's attention. Consider when it is best to play with your child and how to take turns with this. Find ten minutes each day to do this.

Write your diaries for this step, one for difficult times and one for positive times. As in Step 1 these diaries can be used to identify triggers that may lead to a difficult situation (difficult times diary) and those situations which were good and what made them so good (positive times diary).

Recap and review

To recap, the goal, skills and tasks for Step 2 were to understand your child's ADHD so you can apply the skills described based on your assessment of your child's difficulties. In Step 2 the goal was about tailoring the strategies to your child's difficulties in your role as your child's trainer.

Skills summary for Step 2

The skills we covered were:

1. starting to use scaffolding and scoping what your child can do
2. finding teachable moments
3. earshotting
4. adopting a consistent routine
5. giving clear behaviour boundaries, house rules
6. using countdowns and delay fading
7. learning to give clear messages (remember eye contact)
8. using short sentences
9. using choices, preferably two
10. avoiding rows, using negotiation
11. keeping calm yourself
12. calming your child.

The tasks for Step 2 reviewed

The tasks we covered in this step were:

- to continue to work together with partner
- remembering to keep trying skills out over and over again
- learning to manage behaviour while being realistic about what you can achieve
- remembering to practice skills from Step 1, e.g. eye contact, listening and praise
- starting to play games to help improve your child's attention
- playing together for at least ten minutes a day
- keeping a diary for difficult times
- keeping a diary for positive times.

Assessing your child's abilities

We would like you to sit with your child and watch him with either a jigsaw or pack of cards. If you are using a jigsaw choose one with a small number of pieces, and if you are using cards choose picture cards and start with just a few cards (see 'Snap' above) and get them to match the cards that are the same.

Use the columns below to assess your child's abilities over the next week. Make notes under the headings.

Review Sheet

Date	What are you playing e.g. pairs, Snap	How many cards do you think they can manage?	Did your child manage these?	Did they require help?

Making review notes like this is called *scoping your child's abilities*. We have chosen toys on this occasion for you to practice but scoping can also be done for everyday situations like assessing your child's use of a knife and fork or for assessing how long they can wait (see the example of headings for this below). Use your notebook to compose your own review sheets.

Date	What did Your child want?	How long did they manage to wait until they received it?	Did they require help – use of timer for example?

Assess what your child can do easily now, and then extend this either by increasing the number of jigsaw pieces or cards, for example, or by increasing the time on the timer that he has to wait for something he wants.

Once your child has mastered the new waiting time how or use the new toy pieces (he needs to do this a few times so he has really learnt the skill) then you can increase the task again. Always increase the task in small steps for example one extra jigsaw piece, two extra cards or thirty seconds extra on the timer.

It is important when extending a task that you help your child at first. This enables him to keep trying. If your child becomes upset, go back to a previous task he did easily. The aim is to build his self-esteem, and failing to do something a number of times will not help with this. Leave the extended task a couple of days and try again, perhaps in a different way.

Do not be tempted to push your child on too quickly. He needs to learn the new skill well, and sometimes this can take time. ADHD children tend to rush things and then forget. Doing something well over and over again will help your child to remember the task. We call this *consolidating*. It is also important to try the new skill out in different situations so that the child does not just associate it with the home for example (use *teachable moments*, and thus generalizing the task to other settings).

Diary for good days

Date . . . .

Time . . . .

What made it good? . . . .

. . . .

. . . .

. . . .

What did you do? . . . .

. . . .

. . . .

. . . .

Did it help? . . . .

. . . .

. . . .

. . . .

. . . .

How do you feel now? . . . .

. . . .

. . . .

. . . .

Diary for difficult days

Date . . . .

Time . . . .

Trigger . . . .
. . . .

What Happened? . . . .
. . . .

What did you do? . . . .
. . . .
. . . .

Did it help? . . . .
. . . .
. . . .

How do you feel now? . . . .
. . . .

Would you do anything different? . . . .
. . . .
. . . .
. . . .

STEP *3*

Helping your Child's Attention and Concentration through Play

Goal for Step 3

The aim of this step is to help your child learn to concentrate and pay attention through the use of games and play.

Skills overview for Step 3

The skills you will practice during this step are:

1. recognising the importance of play

2. using attention-training play

3. encouraging listening skills

4. using 'we' and 'I'

5. discussion of emotions and extending your child's language

6. practicing giving your child choices.

Tasks overview for Step 3

The tasks you will carry out later in this step are:

- review the skills from the previous steps

- review the tasks from the previous steps

- use the diaries to see what went well and what did not, and why this might be

- play with your child

- remind yourself to praise yourself for how well you have done

- remind yourself how important you are, as your child's guide and trainer

- reflect on your child's behaviours and how they fit into what you know about ADHD

- practice instructions in different situations to increase your child's compliance (willingness to do what he is told when asked)

- review how your child's play is progressing

- to continue to keep diaries for difficult and good times.

How have the past two steps gone?

Do you think that you and your child are getting on better? Have you remembered to stop and think about his behaviour and how it might be linked to ADHD? Are you praising yourself and the other adults who look after your child for the hard work you are doing trying to change things? Are you using the diaries to review both good and difficult times?

Remember we want to help your child respect you and learn to do what you have asked him to do. *This means that you have to show him respect also.* Getting him to do what you want is a task you have to learn to negotiate together.

Skill 1: Recognizing the importance of play

This step's focus is on play. Play is especially important for children who are ADHD, as they often miss out on areas of play which are vital to development, as they are too busy, or their concentration span is too short.

The play ideas in this manual have been specially selected to help improve your child's concentration, attention and listening skills. You may come across other games yourself which you find work particularly well with your child. If you do, write them in your diary and use them again in the future when choosing games for you and your child to play.

Playing is a good way to learn to have fun together as well as an excellent way of teaching your child to wait his turn, learn to win and lose, and learn to improve his ability to concentrate and pay attention.

Children with ADHD have poor concentration and will need encouragement to get them playing. This will be valuable in improving their concentration levels. They need rapidly rewarding games – games that do not take more than a few minutes to set up, otherwise they will have lost interest. Games involving taking turns help children to learn to wait. Why not try some of the following?

- *Role-play games* – such as using toy cars and a road mat to help with road safety skills.

- Use *Lego* people to help teach life or social skills, such as how we join in games and how to express feelings.

- *Reading stories* and looking at the pictures and individual letters in books will lay down some basic skills for reading as well as help your child concentrate. This will help your child prepare for school. Research suggests that many ADHD children may be disadvantaged in their early school years if they have not learnt the basic appearance of some letters, shapes and the general construction of simple words. Try to spend some time with books. The local library will be useful; the staff often run 'reading together' sessions and other events to encourage young children to develop a fondness for books.

- Reading books together can also be a focus for *developing stories together* 'What comes next do you think, what will happen to the boy? What is he thinking? Does he feel happy? What makes him happy, what makes him sad?'

Playing with your child helps his development. It develops his curiosity and this in turn helps him learn. When you play with your child use language to describe what is happening. That way your child's language skills increase and their ability to express themselves improves.

Children with ADHD have difficulties with attention, impulsivity, and hyperactivity. We mentioned earlier that children with ADHD have an active brain too. Therefore, these children may also have difficulties with their short-term memory and thinking. Your child may not be good at listening before he responds. He may interrupt conversations and his use of social language and understanding of situations may be poor.

Joint play with your child will help your child begin to value sitting quietly, listening to stories and conversation, taking turns, and valuing other people's points of view.

📌 Basic tips about play

- Let your child initiate the play i.e. let him choose which game to play, which book to read.

- Follow his direction – don't lead. Try not to tell your child what to do or take over the game. Don't ask too many questions, this disrupts his concentration as he has to think of an answer. For example, don't say 'What colour is that? or 'What are we making?' all the time.

- Don't devalue aimless play, if it is something that fascinates your child, then it is important he knows you respect his interests.

- If your child has difficulty with play, you should guide him, but try not to direct him too much. This should be his time with you, not when you impose your ideas on him.

- Children make up their own rules when playing. Try to go along with this.

Helping to improve your child's behaviour through play

It may seem too simple, but play is a really good way of helping your child learn. Often as parents we do not seem to find the time to play with our children. By playing with them we can also give them the message that we want to spend time with them and enjoy their company. Children so often look delighted when an adult joins with them in play.

Teaching your child to play and take turns and negotiate helps him learn to get on with friends and the rest of the family. Help your child learn to play for longer periods by using language to expand his ideas. Describing what he is doing often helps prolong play and adds to your child's enjoyment. *Play helps children learn to express their feelings rather than having to act them out.*

Children with ADHD often rush through play and as a result don't learn how to play well. Play is very important to children as it helps them learn about all aspects of life, including how to interact with other people and so improve their social skills and make friends.

Play can take many forms, from imaginative play to educational play. It is important that children have the opportunity to benefit from as many types of play as possible. Listed below are some hints and tips on how to encourage your child's play and in turn improve his concentration.

✒ Further tips about play

- Follow your child's lead – let him choose what he wants to play.
- Pace the play at your child's developmental level. Don't expect too much.
- Do not compete (you are an adult who has already acquired this skill, he has not).
- Engage in role-play and make-believe with your child.
- Laugh and have fun.
- Reward quiet play with your attention.
- Praise and encourage your child's ideas and creativity; don't criticize or directly tell him what to play.
- Do not give too much help. Encourage your child's problem solving.
- Tell your child when you have enjoyed playtime with him.

Here are some questions and expressions we have heard from other parents about play:

Why play with my child?

What is play?

Do I have to play?

I don't know how to play with my child.

I find it boring.

I don't have time, it's so time-consuming.

I am too exhausted to play.

For many parents play is seen as a session of somewhat repetitive, boring and thankless activity. With children with ADHD, play may well be an additional effort because we know that these children have more difficulty concentrating. They flit from one activity to another, and play sessions may sometimes feel unsatisfactory to everyone.

Below we will explain how play can help you and your child. In time, play will become fun.

Why play with your child?

You will learn a lot about your child and yourself during play. Playtime gives your child the message 'you are worthwhile' and 'you are a valuable person'. It makes your child feel special. If you are not focusing your attention on your child when you play, however, your child will soon know that you have 'switched off'.

Play, believe it or not, can be therapeutic for parents too. When you have had a few play sessions with your child you will start to enjoy it and may find it relaxing rather than taxing.

Bringing up children is hard work, especially today when everyone leads such demanding lives. We are busy and often tired. We buy toys and games that children can play with alone. Aside from the expense, no toy or game can act as a substitute for the personal attention of a parent.

We may have forgotten how to play, we may not have had a good model ourselves as a child; it may be difficult to think of ideas for play (see *Ideas List* below). Therefore joint play feels even more difficult to do. With practise and time you will appreciate that joint play is one of the best investments a parent can make. Through playing together you show early on that you are interested in your child, which will help them develop good self-esteem. It will also teach your child vast amounts about:

- communication
- listening
- concentration, attention and working memory
- problem solving
- coordination

- imitation
- creativity
- following directions
- play skills (with others)
- exploration (recognizing smells, texture such as hard or soft, or directions left and right)
- bonding: improving your special relationship with your child
- social skills (listening, talking, communication, meaning, negotiations, taking turns, sharing, cooperation, friendship and how to resolve conflict)
- awareness of self, others, nature, animals, music, rhythm
- observation
- thinking skills
- independence
- fun!

Play really does help children with ADHD. If you are not already doing so, playing with your child is going to be very beneficial.

Sitting together watching TV may be a pleasant time. However, it does not generate much interaction between you and your child. For a child, watching TV is a passive experience with limited benefits when it comes to socialization and self-development. By discussing the television programme with your child, and asking him what happened, what might happen next, was the little boy scared and so on, you can make it into a more interactive experience.

When you begin to play with your child, you may have big ideas about what toys would be best. *Remember to start small and keep play simple.* It is best to try to adapt what you already have around the house. There is no need to go out and spend lots of money; your attention is worth significantly more than any expensive toy. First, do not set yourself up to fail by embarking on a complicated game/ toy or idea. *If the play idea takes time to set up, your child's concentration may have run out before you have everything ready, and you will be left feeling rejected and discouraged from trying again.*

Take the example of *painting*. Any paint work should be done with the quickest paint set, only requiring paint, brush, water, paper, some protective paper for the table and your child's apron. Do not attempt to buy individual colour paints that need mixing and take time to prepare. Consider this at a later stage when your child has begun to have fun from painting and can paint for longer.

Try to encourage your child to concentrate and attend to play by talking to him about what he is doing and making it interesting and thus expanding the play. As he learns to concentrate and attend more to play your child will gain more pleasure from play. He will gradually appreciate that sitting down and playing can be fun and he will want to do more. It is important to make positive comments about the play and not to make any suggestions that what he is doing is not good enough. Don't say 'but that does not look like a horse' which will sound negative to the child. Saying something like 'you have drawn a brown horse' is better. You could even say something like 'Remember we saw horses last week when we walked down the road and you gave them names'. This expands the conversation, suggesting to the child that it can be fun to draw horses, that you are interested in what he has done, *and* you draw on a past situation and connect his painting with something you did together which in turn, helps him remember.

Some children do not like playing on their own. Showing your child how to achieve results from play, like building or making up games, by taking an interest in what he is doing and praising him and encouraging him, will expand his possibilities for play and keep him interested.

Play ideas

Painting

Drawing with pencils or crayons

Cutting paper shapes (Safety and supervision required at all times)

Painting by number

Lego

Bricks or building blocks

Cars

Dolls

Books

Glue and making things

What's in fashion? (e.g. Ben 10, Thomas the Tank Engine, Charlie and Lola)

Any hobbies? (e.g. football, cricket)

Cooking: start simply (Remember to do it when you have energy, as the kitchen will have to be cleaned afterwards.)

Music, singing and rhythm

Poetry and rhymes

Games – such as board games

What is in season? Make Christmas cards, trimmings, birthday cards, a Valentine card, Easter cards

Playing in the sand pit

Swimming

Dressing up

Pretend play – shop, schools, house keeping, cooking, doctors and nurses

Gardening – e.g. pulling weeds, looking at flowers, watering the plants, planting flowers from seeds

Add other ideas that you have here: ....

....

....

....

Coming up with play ideas can be difficult. The library has many books on play. School staff may give you some ideas as they are continually making things with the children and could remind you of events coming up of interest. For example, for the different festivities and holidays you can make decorations and cards, at Halloween you can make scary masks.

Other family members may also be asked about any tips on play. Having a list of play ideas nearby (for you) can help, especially when you are feeling tired and cannot think of a play idea. You could add your own ideas when you see or think of something that would be helpful.

Skill 2: Attention-training play

All play is beneficial towards children's development however children with ADHD may have specific difficulties so the games below have been developed through research for their impact on children's attention and concentration. We have found that children's ability to concentrate and pay attention often increases when they practice these with their parents for ten minutes each day.

The reason we have suggested and researched these games is because they are quick, easy and cheap to play. A pack of cards, for example, is not expensive to buy. Cards can be carried in your pocket and played with in and out of the home.

Games will help your child's *visual memory* (Snap, Pairs, and Kim's Game) and some will help his *auditory memory* (I spy, Simon says, I went to market and I bought (or I went to the zoo and I saw etc). They also help concentration and attention and listening skills.

Scope your child to decide how many cards you can use for example for snap or pairs and as he gets the hang of it increase the number being used. The games also teach turn taking, are fun, and can be completed with everyone feeling in a win-win situation. As they are over quickly if the child loses, you can play again and tell him that he may win next time. *Remember to keep talking as the game begins to encourage your child to stay interested. Agree on the rules before you start playing (that includes with any adults too!)*

Snap

You started playing this in the second week (Step 2)

See p. 80 for instructions.

This game is useful for teaching your child to concentrate, take turns, work on his visual memory and cope with losing. The beauty of this game is that as it is a very quick game to play, and finish, the child knows that a new game happens quickly.

Pairs

This game helps attention training, listening, taking turns, and waiting. This builds on the skills learnt from playing Snap. It extends the ability of the child to remember pictures.

Take some cards in pairs (say five pairs to start with); picture ones are best. Place them face down on the floor or a table, and scatter them around. The aim is to find the matching pairs. In turn, turn over one then a second card. When you find the matching pair remove it from the floor. If the pair does not match turn back face down in the same place on the table or floor. The object is to try to remember where on the floor the pairs are. The player with the most pairs wins. Encourage your child to remember where the cards are on the floor. Remember to praise him for waiting his turn, and concentrating on the game. Praise him when he finds a pair. *Remember this is your child's chance to win, not yours; it is not a competition with your child.*

Play can be developed further by taking opportunities to match pairs or groups of objects when you are out and about, such as cars of the same colour, same make, same size (grabbing teachable moments).

Kim's Game

Put two items onto a tray or in a box. Get the child to look at them, and then cover the items up. Then ask your child to re-member what was there. Increase the number of items gradually as your child becomes better at it.

This simple but effective game works on listening skills and visual and auditory memory.

I went to market

Taking turns, one of you starts off: 'I went to market and I bought a loaf of bread'. The next person has to say the same sentence, remember the loaf of bread and one other item, and then the next person goes through the same list adding his item, and so on. This will build up the child's auditory and word memory and help listening skills. You can make it fun by buying funny items.

You can change it to 'I went to the Zoo [...]' and I saw an elephant then a giraffe or 'I went to the park' and I saw a swing and so on.

Games like this one can be played when waiting for buses, on train journeys, at Granny's (teachable moments).

I spy

This is a useful game to keep children quiet in the car or on a bus journey, or when they are tired on a walk. It helps them to look around them and take an interest. Remember to make it simple at first so your child understands the rules.

So the parent will say: 'I spy with my little eye, something beginning with D, or something red, or something you can write with [...].'

Plan the game at the child's level of skill. Then it is the child's turn.

Simon Says

This is a good game to make children learn to wait and to listen. When you say 'Simon says walk two steps', the child is allowed to walk, if you just say 'walk two steps', the child stays still. You can vary it with 'Simon says make a funny face' or anything that makes it fun. This game will help your child's auditory memory, as well as his listening and attending skills.

Remember when you are playing a game to set a time limit. This is important so that you know how long you are playing for so you can concentrate and not think of all the other tasks you have to do. Setting a time limit is also important so that the game has a beginning and an ending and you both keep to it. It is more useful for your child to play for frequent short periods of time than only one long time that ends in tears. *You could use a timer.*

Reviewing your child's progress with play

Once you have played these games a few times with your child, you should start using a play review sheet to assess his progress and make sure you are extending his learning appropriately.

The play diary example we give below is in two sections. The first is aimed at play using the specific attention and concentration games we have suggested to you such as Snap, Pairs, I went to market. Using the guide below should help you *scope* your child's abilities over time and keep a check on how he is progressing.

Assess your child's abilities over the next week and note the following:

Review sheet for attention-training games

Date	What are you playing e.g. Pairs	How many cards do you think he can manage?	Did your child manage these?	Did he require help?

When you have filled in these play review sheets, make your own in your notepad. The review sheet below is for play that your child chooses including drawing, painting and so on – see the list on p.96

Review sheet for play activities

Date	Type of play e.g. painting	How long did he play for?	Were there any difficulties?	What went well?

Quality time

Play is a form of quality time. Try to encourage good quality time (stories, games etc) between you and your child.

What exactly is quality time? Many people believe that quality time has to be action-packed time. This is not true. Quality time with your child can be whatever you want it to be. It could be having a cuddle together, reading a book or playing a game together. Just talking, listening or maybe having some quiet time together. Sharing things together, making tea, going out together.

Children need to know that they are loved and wanted and that you are prepared to spend and enjoy spending time with them. *Do not let bad behaviour be the only way that your child gets attention from you.*

Skill 3: Encouraging listening skills

How do you get your child to do what you have asked him to do?

We have discussed helping your child to listen to you so that he can hear what you want him to do. We have talked about how important it is that your child knows that you are pleased with the good behaviour he has shown.

We have talked about how the way you talk to your child and the way you ask him to do something are important. Practice these essential listening skills as much as you can.

Skill 4: 'WE' and 'I' and tone of voice

Enthusiasm in your voice is very important, especially when presenting two choices, since you can use it to highlight the choice that you really want him to make. Speak to your child as you would like to be spoken to. How would you, the adult address a friend, for example? Speak at the level of understanding of the child.

Speak in a socially correct manner. Start by understanding that if you say 'please' and 'thank you' yourself in appropriate situations, the child will follow your example (mirror image again). Remind yourself that respect is taught, and children will not know how to express it automatically.

Use 'we' for house rules such as, 'We walk in this house,' 'We are gentle with people and animals,' 'We sit on the furniture, we do not jump on furniture,' 'We shut doors quietly'.

Try if you can to use positive house rules rather than negative ones, for example: 'We shut the door quietly', rather than 'Do not bang the door'.

Draw, paint or write the house rules and display them on the wall. This helps you and your child to remember the agreed rules and they can be used when other children visit. The rules should apply to all children in your house.

When you come across a particularly difficult problem with your child's behaviour try to build a strategy around the problem into the house rules. Make sure that it is attainable and not unrealistic. Eventually when you go out visiting all that you need to say is 'We know the house rules'.

To recap, by using 'we', we:

- protect our child's self-esteem

- take the pressure off him and make it less likely that he will refuse to stick to acceptable behaviour.

For example, 'We do not do..... here,' 'When you are calm we can talk about it.'

Skill 5: Discussing emotions and extending your child's use of language

Children often have difficulty explaining why they are cross. It is important to help them learn to put emotions into words. Children with ADHD in particular often have problems learning to express themselves and have problems with self regulation.

For example, sometimes children become cross when asked to do something as they often don't know how to do it. Instead of being able to explain that, they shout or have a temper tantrum. Parents can help their child to learn to share their feelings by talking to their child about times when they have not known what to do or have felt frustrated. This should encourage the child to share rather than act out.

Use the 'I' message. For example, 'When you did... I felt happy.' 'When you did... I felt sad.' Use broad and clear messages avoiding if possible the words good and bad, because your child will not understand what behaviour was good or bad. Explain in simple words what the acceptable or unacceptable action was. This is particularly important as it also introduces children to the concept of having feelings and we hope that over time it will help your child to be able to express his feelings better.

Skill 6: Choices revisited

Remember to keep choices which avoid a 'no' answer. This takes practice for parents and eventually if you do practise it will become automatic. For example, 'Do you want play a game of cards now or later on after lunch?' Change 'no' to 'yes' whenever possible. 'Yes you can have a... after tea. Yes, we will go to the park after we...' If you are already carrying out many of the above approaches keep up the good work.

Tasks for Step 3

Take some time to review the skills and tasks from the previous steps. How are these going? Are you using the diaries to review difficult and positive times?

Remember to put aside time to play with your child. Ten minutes each day helps. You can use the timer to signify the start and end of the play time. Are you and your partner working together in your approach to your child in order to provide him with the consistency he needs because of his ADHD characteristics? Remember to praise yourself mentally when you handle a situation well. If you feel confident with a skill in the home start to try it in different situations.

Remember to keep using the diaries.

Your own memories of childhood

We know that disciplining a difficult child is extremely hard work and that it may bring out memories and flashbacks from your own childhood. How your parents used to discipline you, and how you remember this, could bring back unpleasant or disturbing memories for you.

If this happens you may want to discuss this with someone. Your health visitor or doctor may be able to advise you about whom to contact, if you ask them. Don't try to carry on without help if you are finding this aspect troubling.

It is essential to work on building your own self-confidence in your ability to instil boundaries for your child. Many parents when managing a child with ADHD may have low self-esteem. You may have lost your confidence, as other people keep commenting that your child's difficult behaviour is your fault and making you feel inadequate. Try and choose someone you trust to help you. It could be a partner, friend, parent or a health professional.

Recap and review

Goal for Step 3

The goal for this step was to help your child learn to concentrate and pay attention through the use of games.

Skills summary for Step 3

The skills you acquired in this step were:

1. the importance of playing with your child
2. attention-training play
3. encouraging listening skills

4.   using 'we' and 'I'

5.   discussing emotions and extending language

6.   using choices.

Tasks summary for Step 3

The tasks you practiced were:

- reviewing the skills from the previous steps

- reviewing the tasks from the previous steps

- using the diaries to see what went well and what did not, and why this might be

- playing with your child

- praising yourself for how well you have done

- reminding yourself how important you are, as your child's guide and trainer

- reflecting on your child's behaviour and how it fits into what you know about ADHD

- practicing more situations to increase your child's compliance (his willingness to do what he is told without a fuss)

- continuing to keep diaries for difficult and good times.

You have now completed the first three steps in the programme – well done. There is a lot of information in each of the steps. You should be gaining confidence as you go through each step. Remember children will challenge any change in your behaviour as parents. Stick with it – it does help in the end.

Diary for good days

Date . . . .

Time . . . .

What made it good? . . . .

. . . .

. . . .

. . . .

What did you do? . . . .

. . . .

. . . .

. . . .

Did it help? . . . .

. . . .

. . . .

. . . .

. . . .

How do you feel now? . . . .

. . . .

. . . .

. . . .

Diary for difficult days

Date . . . .

Time . . . .

Trigger . . . .

. . . .

What Happened? . . . .

. . . .

. . . .

What did you do? . . . .

. . . .

. . . .

Did it help? . . . .

. . . .

. . . .

How do you feel now? . . . .

. . . .

. . . .

Would you do anything different? . . . .

. . . .

. . . .

. . . .

Step **4**

Improving your Child's Communication

Goal for Step 4

The goal for this step is to help your child with his communication skills to enable him to express his feelings and learn to manage his behaviour.

Skills overview for Step 4

The skills you will acquire during this step are:

1. expanding your child's language through play

2. working on voice (e.g. volume and tone)

3. setting clear goals and expectations

4. how to deal with temper tantrums and using distraction techniques

5. anticipation

6. the concept of quiet time

7. time out

8. cueing your child to tasks and changes of task (Step 2)

9. coping with delay

10. talking about and showing feelings.

Tasks overview for Step 4

The tasks you will carry out in the course of the fourth step in the programme are:

- review your progress and difficulties from Steps 1–3

- remember your role as guide and trainer

- recall how important you are as a positive role model for your child

- find opportunities for play (quality time)

- find more teachable moments.

Skill 1: Expanding your child's language through play

Try to put aside time each day to play the games we suggested in Step 3 and enjoy your time together in other ways, such as reading stories, painting, going for walks, whatever you and your child find to do that works for the pair of you. Remember if you talk to your child while you are playing, and praise and encourage him, you will be helping him to feel good about himself. By using descriptive comments and explanations to extend play you are encouraging him to keep playing and get something out of it.

For example, during your child's bath time when you may be playing with toy ducks you might say 'Do you remember when we fed the ducks?'… Or 'We saw ducks when we were with Granny'… whatever is appropriate. By using language, you keep the child interested in carrying on playing, as the play has additional meaning.

Skill 2: Working on tone of voice

In the last step we discussed using 'I' statements. The tone of voice you use will also enable your child to understand what you mean. A firm tone of voice highlights you mean what you say. Praise and a positive tone of voice will give the impression to your child that you are proud of him and his behaviour.

We have talked about using language and the 'I' and 'we' words but also how you say things is very important. Children often pick up more from your tone of voice than what you are saying. Below are some more thoughts on tone of voice.

1. Your voice should remain as calm as possible in difficult situations.

2. Remember to smile when saying something positive; remember to smile with your eyes also. Children look into eyes and if the expression in your eyes does not match the one on the rest of your face your child may not know whether you are really happy with him.

3. Your child will watch you and your expressions – check them out yourself in a mirror. What do you look like when you're happy, sad or angry? Does your child look similar when he is happy, sad or angry? Is this how you want him to feel and act?

4. Try to end the day on a positive note. Spend time reminding your child all the good things he has done that day. If he can, get him to tell you the good things he has done too. This helps him to reinforce the good and encourage more of the same behaviour.

Skill 3: Setting clear goals and expectations

A positive targeted approach to rules and expected behaviour will give your child a clear message that you expect him to do what you ask him to do. It is very important to set rules and tasks for him, which he will be able to achieve. Try to work out what he can do, and set realistic goals. Remember to try to see this as a win-win situation for both you and your child.

If you have observed that your child can sit and play for five minutes, praise him for doing that. Then next time expect him to sit for six minutes and then praise him for doing so. If you know your child can manage to put on his pants and vest without a prompt, praise him for that, and then ask him to put on his shirt too before you come back and then praise him for what he has achieved. If your child can manage to wait for his turn to speak for half a minute, praise him, and then next time, help him to wait for one whole minute. *In this way, we are helping you to encourage your child to build up his skills and his ability to solve problems for himself.*

Skill 4: Temper tantrums and distraction techniques

Intervene before a tantrum happens, if possible. Work out what causes the temper tantrum, and when you see it happening, quickly distract the child onto something else. For example, your child is about to have a major wobbly because his younger brother has taken his toy, so you intervene before he does. Have a list of strategies in the back of your mind that could be used for distraction (practice them or write them down).

Use voice appropriately. Make your tone exciting, signalling enthusiasm in the words that you are using to distract. Make what you are suggesting fun and hard for the child to say 'no'.

For example, say 'I know that it is not fair that…. has taken your toy'

'…but let's play with this car' or

'…here is some more Lego' or

'…I will make sure you both have enough crayons to play with' or

'Wow, look at… is it a bird, I wonder what colour it is? Can you see him and then tell me?' (to help distract him) or

'You can draw beautiful pictures. Shall I help you to get started?'

Skill 5: Anticipation

It is not always easy to predict when things may be difficult, but understanding how your child views the world can help you anticipate situations which he may find difficult. Sometimes using the diaries can help you identify triggers. Many parents notice that their child's behaviour is often worse when he is tired or hungry. It may be easier to lower your expectations of your child at these times, ignoring minor misbehaviour.

If you know your child can usually manage five minutes of play before getting cross or wanting to 'borrow' his brother's toys, then watch and encourage him for playing well for that length of time. If you then see he is about to want his brother's toys, discuss with him how he could negotiate that, or use language to help him play longer with the toys he is already playing with for example by describing what he is doing or what could happen next.

If your child is about to lose his temper, use the distraction techniques that you have thought of. Note which one seems to work best with your child.

If your child has problems playing with others it is important that you try to be in the same room with him so you can intervene early. By doing this you will gradually teach your child the art of negotiation so that he will learn to control his temper. As he acquires this skill he will get better at playing independently with his friends. As you become more attuned to your child, you will begin to recognize when he is likely to have a temper tantrum, and you will gradually be able to manage these situations with quiet time (discussed next).

Skill 6: Quiet time

Quiet time is a technique to help your child learn to self-regulate his behaviour. This means that over time your child will learn when he is likely to get into trouble or difficulty and give himself time to calm down.

In the first instance we ask that you use the diaries to identify triggers for difficult situations, for example your child may be able to play with a friend for 15 minutes without any difficulties, but if you leave him for longer then they start to row. If you see signs that your child is getting wound up, then ask him at about 12 minutes to come to the 'quiet time mat'. On this mat are some quiet toys. Tell him he can play with them until he has calmed down and then he can return to playing with his friend. You should stay with him next to his mat – *this is not a punishment.* The quiet place should be viewed as a positive zone to give you both time to calm down and to stop situations escalating out of control.

You and your child should discuss when you will use quiet time. For example, use it if you think that your child is about to lose his temper, or if it is clear that a game is getting too noisy and it will end in a fight if not stopped. Quiet time is ideal if your child when playing a game starts thinking that it is 'not fair' and cannot continue without a getting into a temper. *Remember it is important to try to help your child reach a stage when he begins to recognize the need for a period of quiet time himself.*

How to use quiet time or talk your child down

If you can see that your child is about to lose his temper and get cross, withdraw with him to a place that you have already discussed, a step or a quiet place or a mat, that is easily transportable or transferable to different settings. *Talk your child down* – calm him before something happens. If you can, this will teach your child to negotiate. Sometimes you can use recollected films you have enjoyed for the child to imagine he is in a magic place and then he can visualize a happy, tranquil scene in order to calm himself down. Use the same techniques that you would use yourself such as breathing slowly and deeply and counting to ten. Your child can be allowed to take two toys with him – playing quietly will help. The purpose is for your child to become calm and gradually begin to recognize in himself the signs when he is getting cross. You can talk to him when he is calm about what he might have done differently, for example, sharing toys, using language to negotiate sharing.

A mat (a small piece of carpet, e.g. a carpet square from a carpet shop or even a square of material) is useful as it can be taken out to Granny's or used in playgroup, and school. The mat needs to be introduced prior to using it for quiet time or talk down, so the child understands what is expected and why it should not be seen as a punishment. It is like a *magic carpet for using for quiet time.*

A parent can also use quiet time for space for her- or him-self when she or he thinks events may become fraught and she needs time away from her child. (Make sure your child is safe, or another adult is available to look after him.) Quiet time, then, can be used as a modelling example from parent to child. You could say 'Do you remember when mummy was cross she went outside to sit on the step to calm down?' This will help your child learn by example. It is also helpful for you to discuss when your own quiet time might be used with your child, so he knows when you are likely to need space.

With an older child one can say 'We need a period of quiet time. You sit there and I will sit over here. When we are both calm we can have a cuddle and we will talk about what happened'. If you feel that you are getting really cross with your child then it might better for both of you to be in different rooms to calm down.

You can use the house rules to demonstrate to your child what is expected of him and have the consequences drawn up in advance – so both parent and child know what to expect and what will happen. If your child has done something which is against the house rules for example, he has hit his sister or brother, you then might need to use 'time out'. We explain below where time out and quiet time might be used and the difference in the ideas.

Skill 7: Time out

Time out is a more extreme measure than quiet time and should only be used as a last resort when distraction, quiet time, presenting your child with choices and other strategies have not worked, and the child's behaviour is unacceptable. It should be used as little as possible, as the aim of this step-by-step programme is to help the child learn to control his behaviour. Time out can however be useful in setting firm boundaries around totally unacceptable behaviour such as hitting others. You and your child should decide beforehand what would merit time out, for example hitting another child or parent, throwing things, becoming destructive. This could be written in the house rules as a reminder alongside more positive rules such as rewards for good behaviour.

How to use time out

If your child's behaviour is such that you need to use time out, you would first warn the child. Say to him that he will have to go to time out if the behaviour does not stop immediately. You can use counting one... two... three, if this will work for your child. But only use one, two, and three if time out is the sanction.

Time out is used when your child has done something that is not acceptable. Use a step, or a chair or his room if the child will accept this (some children see being sent to their room as rejection and make such a fuss that it becomes unhelpful). If necessary carry the child to time out if he will not go himself. Make sure your child knows the situations when time out would be used and where it is going to take place.

The duration of time out should be one minute for each year of your child's age to a maximum of ten minutes. If your child comes out from time out take him back and stay with him, if he cannot stay on his own, but with minimal contact and no discussion until the time is up. If your child has a sensitive temperament (see Chapter 2, p. 29) staying on his own is very difficult for him. He may need the reassurance of an adult nearby. It is important however that discussion and interaction should be kept to a minimum at this time.

Time out should be used as a last resort if all the other strategies haven't worked. If it is happening too often, then you should review your house rules with your child, as it may be that by going back over why things are going wrong, you might lessen the need for time out. Some children respond better when parents reinforce house rules and boundaries at the beginning of each day. This sends the message that the parents are in charge and can manage their child's behaviour. If your child responds to frequent repetition and statement of boundaries then being firm at the beginning of the day may reduce the need for time out.

Sometimes you do need to withdraw your child from a situation as nothing else is working. Sometimes you two need time apart in order to calm down. If you think you need time apart ask your partner or friend to help out. Remember it can take you time to calm down.

✦ Tips on dealing with temper tantrums
Here are some ideas for what to do if they've lost it!
- Keep calm, ignore your child's extreme behaviour if possible (remember to use the *perspex screen* p. 77).
- Do not discuss the incident, if the child is in the throes of an outburst he is not listening or able to listen.

- Give him time to calm down.
- Give yourself time to calm down. *It takes the adult brain 20 minutes of time out to calm down.*
- Discuss what could have been done differently with your child at a later point.

Skill 8: Cueing your child into tasks and changes of task

We talked in Step 2 about using countdowns into a change of task or situation. For example rather than just telling your child it is time to leave for school, remind your child that you have to go out in a few minutes (remembering to cue him down in five minutes, in four minutes as necessary), then remind him at one minute that he will have to stop playing and get his coat and shoes. This gives your child a chance to prepare for, and accept, a change. *Remember children with ADHD may not like change.*

Keep practicing this skill, and gradually practise cueing in less when your child becomes better at making the adjustments for regular, everyday, tasks. Use the technique especially for new situations, or when your child is tired or you have a series of tasks to do like a complicated morning with shopping in more than one place, or visiting friends. It is always important to cue your child into something you want him to do or something you want him to stop doing.

Skill 9: Coping with delay

Helping your child learn to wait is important as many aspects of everyday life require waiting and many children with ADHD find this difficult. You can start by helping your child learn to wait for lunch or a biscuit, or until you have finished doing something. Increase the time he has to wait for things gradually. *We call this delay fading,* as we saw in Step 2. You can use the timer for this.

It is important for children with ADHD to work on their ability to wait, and to become aware of their dificulties, so ask your child 'How long do you think you can wait for...today?' so he sets his own targets for waiting. You may have to modify these if you do not think he will manage to wait that long. This is part of the scoping you undertake with your child (see Step 2) as it is important that he succeeds and he is then praised for being able to wait.

Helping the child learn to wait will improve his ability to wait his turn when playing games and waiting for instructions thus helping the child improve his relationships with peers and adults. It will also lesson the impulsivity of some children with ADHD so they learn to wait instead of running off or butting into conversations.

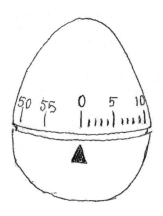 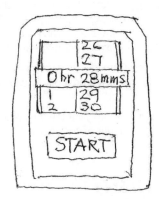

Skill 10: Talking about and showing feelings

Listen carefully when your child talks to you.

Encourage your child to tell you how he feels. Notice how he seems to be feeling and say to him when he looks happy or sad. Being able to communicate feelings helps the child and stops him from acting out his feelings instead.

It can often help children if you explain what you are feeling and why – not necessarily in detail but enough so he can understand your point of view. Children often blame themselves if parents are in a bad mood – they think they must have done something to cause it, when it may be that you have just received a bill you were not expecting. Explaining to your child helps him to know when you are upset and why. *Remember to do this when you are happy too.*

Keep a diary and note any difficulties carrying out the above skills. Remember to keep a diary for positive times too!

📌 Tips on the importance of feelings

- Help your child to discuss his feelings rather than act them out.
- Ask him if he is sad, happy or angry. If you've got it wrong he will tell you.
- If your child learns to tell you his feelings he is less likely to act them out through his temper.
- Acknowledging your child's feelings will help him feel listened to. *Don't be tempted to dismiss his feelings.* They will be real to him even if you do not think they are accurate. You can help him see positives at another time.
- You can give your child ideas to manage his feelings such as punching a pillow when angry or drawing what has made him sad.
- Share your feelings with him too. Find ways of dealing with feelings together.

Tasks for Step 4

Remember to review your progress and difficulties from Steps 1–3. Note those skills and tasks you find easy and those more difficult.

Remember that you are acting as your child's guide and trainer and that you are important as a positive role model for your child.

Keep finding opportunities to play with your child using both attention-training games and free play where you play games of his choice – both are important.

Try to gain confidence in using the skills in different situations: practice and practice until you feel confident.

Recap and review

Goal for Step 4

The objective for this fourth step was for you to help your child with their communication skills to enable him to express his feelings and learn to manage his behaviour better.

Skills summary for Step 4

In this step you practiced the following skills:

1. extending your child's language during play
2. working on your voice (e.g. volume and tone)
3. setting clear goals and expectations
4. learning how to deal with temper tantrums and use distraction techniques
5. anticipation of difficult situations
6. using the concept of quiet time
7. using time out
8. developing how you cue your child into tasks and changes of task
9. helping your child cope with delay
10. talking about and showing feelings.

Tasks summary for Step 4

In this step you carried out the following tasks:

*   you reviewed your progress and difficulties from Steps 1–3
*   you remembered your role as guide and trainer
*   you recalled how important you are as a positive role model for your child
*   you found opportunities for play (quality time)
*   you found teachable moments as in all steps of the programme.

Step 4 can be one of the most challenging for parents. Managing your child's difficult behaviour in a way that he can learn to eventually manage himself, is hard. Persevere. Helping your child to learn to regulate his own responses is an extremely important skill for children with ADHD. If this skill is established early on in childhood, it will help your child considerably in his teenage years when children tend to be able to communicate less because of the changes that are happening within their brain and bodies. Ensuring that communication between you and your child is as positive and effective as it can be before he becomes a teenager helps both of you learn to negotiate early on, and can prevent many difficult situations in the future.

Quality time

Quality time is important for parents and children. By quality time we mean time that parents and children spend doing something that both want to do and that is fun. Reading stories together, playing games, painting, cooking – anything that is quiet and fun and not demanding. Parents should try if possible to build sometime during each day for this – it does not have to be for long. Even ten minutes when the child feels that his mother or father is devoting his or her time to him works well.

Diary for good days

Date . . . .

Time . . . .

What made it good? . . . .

    . . . .

    . . . .

    . . . .

What did you do? . . . .

    . . . .

    . . . .

    . . . .

Did it help? . . . .

. . . .

. . . .

. . . .

. . . .

How do you feel now? . . . .

    . . . .

    . . . .

    . . . .

Diary for difficult days

Date . . . .

Time . . . .

Trigger . . . .
. . . .

What Happened? . . . .
. . . .
. . . .

What did you do? . . . .
. . . .
. . . .

Did it help? . . . .
. . . .
. . . .

How do you feel now? . . . .
. . . .

Would you do anything different? . . . .
. . . .
. . . .
. . . .

Step **5**

Managing your ADHD Child Outside of the Home

Goal for Step 5

The aim of this step is for you to apply all the skills you have learnt so far in the programme, and to transfer these into everyday situations outside of the home.

Skills overview for Step 5

The skills you will practice during Step 5 of the programme are:

1. listening, sharing feelings and mutual respect
2. extending the use of timers
3. calming your child outside the home
4. more on earshotting
5. repetition of instructions outside the home
6. using house rules
7. rewards
8. teachable moments in depth.

Tasks overview for Step 5

The tasks you will engage in during this fifth step are:

- use the checklist to see how you are doing

- play games for at least ten minutes each day

- keep diaries for positives and difficult times

- find teachable moments.

Parents checklist – self-monitoring

Before we discuss the skills for Step 5 we introduce a way for you to review those skills you have already learnt in previous steps. There follows a short questionnaire based on the skills we have discussed so far in the programme. By completing this you will be able to see how you are doing in using the ideas we have given you in this self-help manual. Are there some skills and tasks you find easier to do than others? We all tend to avoid doing what we find difficult. Or we may just have forgotten to do some stages in the programme. The questionnaire is a way for you to check for yourself, which things you are doing well, and what needs further practice. It is sometimes helpful to complete this with your partner as you will each have things that you find easier to do, and you may be able to support one another with ideas you find difficult. This is a guide to help you reflect on what you have learnt over the last four steps and to provide you with the chance to see how things are going. Take some time to complete it and think about what it shows. Making changes in your parenting is hard as is changing your child's behaviour, but the questionnaire will show you how much you have achieved already.

Skill 1: Listening, sharing feelings and mutual respect

Learning how to talk with children is perhaps the most important part of child rearing. It will be how your child learns to talk with others and therefore how he is outside the home. All children are

Parent's checklist

		Not at all	A little	Often
1	I remember to get my child's attention before giving instructions			
2	I remember to use eye contact for positives			
3	I am good at giving praise frequently			
4	My partner and I work closely together to manage our child			
5	I am consistent in my approch to my child			
6	I give clear messages to my child			
7	I use countdowns when my child needs to change from what he's doing			
8	I have clear behaviour boundaries			
9	I avoid rows and keep calm, I anticipate difficult times			
10	I practice giving my child limited choices			
11	I use the word 'we' rather than 'you'			
12	I play games with my child to improve his attention for at least ten minutes each day			
13	I have practiced using quiet time with my child			
14	I make sure I speak with the appropriate voice to my child			
15	I talk about how I feel and encourage my child to do the same			
16	I listen to what my child is saying to me			
17	I try to expand his play by describing what he is doing			
18	I manage any outbursts well			
19	I manage to anticipate and distract my child preventing outbursts			
20	I use timers often			
21	I praise my child's behaviour to others (Granny etc)			
22	I remember to repeat instructions to my child			
23	I have clearly displayed house rules			
24	I regularly review my child's ability in order to help him progress (scaffolding)			
25	I regularly reflect on how I am doing as a parent			

born with their own individual personalities. At the same time many environmental factors influence the way a child behaves. The main factors are how you as his parent:

- guide and advise your child

- nurture your child

- establish rules and boundaries, setting limits

- protect your child's feelings and manage their influence on his self-esteem and social skills.

All of the above are carried out through communication, and by example.

The statement 'They will grow out of it!' is often an excuse. Unacceptable behaviour that is not checked will only get worse. It is difficult to control young children however if behaviour is not checked it will be worse when he is older, because the foundations of good communication and boundaries have not been established.

Talking helps to develop language skills and children's ability to express themselves and communicate with other people. Listening to your child develops in your child a sense of being understood and respected. This will help your child feel acknowledged and trusted. It will also make him feel safe. He needs to feel safe enough to be able to tell you when life gets difficult for him, however hard or awful what he recounts may be for you to listen to as a parent. It is at these times that he needs to trust you to help him even if he realizes you may also be cross with him. Learning the skill of listening and paying attention as parents is an art too.

Many families find it very difficult to express in words how they feel. If this is hard for the adult it is near impossible for the child. Many children who have difficulties with their emotions struggle because they do not know the words to describe and make sense of what they are feeling. Your child needs examples and he needs to hear the right words used to describe emotions. He needs to know how to explore emotions using words and ideas pitched at the appropriate developmental stage for your child. It will help if you can use emotion words in your everyday language e.g. 'I feel cross because I can't open this jar'.

Apologize – it is healthy to apologize. If you apologize, your child will learn to say sorry too. It is important to make it clear what you are apologizing for. Ensure that you mean what you say and that your voice tone matches what you are saying. The way you use language with your child at home has a direct and immediate effect on how he will interact with other people outside the home.

Skill 2: Expanding the use of timers

We talked about using timers in the first two steps to help your child learn about the concept of time and to put boundaries around activities.

Timers can be useful for a number of reasons.

- They can help your child learn to wait for something, for example a parent might say when the timer goes off then you can have... (See coping with delay in earlier steps)

- They can help him play for longer and build up his concentration: –'How long do you think you can play with the jigsaw today?'

- They can help your child by providing him with a boundary. They give a start and an ending which is visible. 'See if you can get dressed by the time the timer goes off.'

- They can be used to help your child set his own time, for example a parent may make the statement, 'You know you will have to wait to do that, how long do you think you can wait today?' This helps your child to think about his waiting time and he can be encouraged to increase how long he can wait.

- They give your child the seeds of his understanding of time perception and how long it takes to do things. Remember some children with ADHD have problems with this.

Using the timer can help your child start to learn to regulate himself and understand his own difficulties, as well as providing him with the skills to manage them.

Skill 3: Calming your child outside the home

We have talked about keeping calm and speaking respectfully to your child, and what to do when things are difficult. These are all good techniques to help your child. Children with ADHD tend to be 'always on the go'. Your child may find it hard to relax and sit still for any length of time. To help your child with this, there are some ideas below. Each child is different and relaxation skills can take a while to learn, so you may need to practice them with your child for a while before he gets the hang of them.

Tips on helping your child to relax
- Have a designated quiet time during the day when your child listens to relaxing music or reads quietly.
- Some children like to soak in a warm bath with bubbles.
- Some children like to have their feet massaged.
- Some children like to have their back tickled.
- Lying quietly on the floor while you tell each other stories can be relaxing – as long as the stories are relaxing too!

Children with ADHD are good at being active but they need to learn that not everyone can keep up with them.

Try to identify the activities that most suit your child which he can do to relax. It may be watching TV, having a massage, or listening to music. This is an important skill for him to learn as he often has a great deal of energy so he can exhaust himself and others!

Helping your child relax will help him with friendships and relationships in later life. If your child learns to relax properly at home he will be calmer outside the home too.

It is important to remember that your child needs to know the plan for the day.

If you are planning to go to the supermarket and you know that this can sometimes cause your child to get bored and become cross, then remind him that you have to go shopping. You will be as quick as you can. He can help by getting some of the things for you. If he can be helpful and not get cross then he will have a reward (which you have agreed on before you go). Remember supermarkets are noisy and distracting for young children and your child may find it difficult to go there. Make the trip as short as possible, and encourage good behaviour by keeping him involved.

Try to anticipate when your child is getting cross then try to distract him and encourage him to sit quietly. If he does have a temper tantrum then take him off to one side and if distraction does not work, then sit with him and ignore him, keeping him safe until he stops. If this does not work abandon the shopping and take him back to the car, which you can use for time out.

The most important factors are:

- planning the outing carefully for a time when you and he are not tired

- make it as short as possible

- keep him involved and interested so he does not become bored

- praise good behaviour

- reward at the end

Skill 4: More on earshotting

Previously mentioned in Step 2, this is the simple technique of talking about the positive behaviour your child has demonstrated, when he can hear – to partners, friends or relatives. It is a good way of raising your child's self-esteem while encouraging others to see the good in your child. Children with ADHD are often seen as naughty by other people and this is a good way of ensuring their good points are seen too. Remember to keep doing this when you are outside the home and have the opportunity. It is important for you child to know you think highly of him.

Skill 5: Repetition of instructions

Getting your child to repeat instructions is a good way of reminding him of the task in hand and helping him with his memory. Remember children with ADHD have short-term memory problems. This means your child can often remember what happened months ago, but not what you just asked him to do. If your child seems to have difficulty with this then a good way to help him is to ask him gently to tell you what he has to do, for example 'Is it time to put your shoes on?' Then ask the child 'What did Mummy/Daddy just ask you to do?' Remember instructions should be short. Give no more than one or two instructions at a time. Do not ask your child to repeat what you asked him to do every time, just occasionally, and when it is important for your child to remember something.

Skill 6: House rules and the outside world

As we have seen, these can be very helpful in several ways. They can give you a chance to think about what is really important for your family to stick to. They also give you a chance to discuss with others who live in the household what is important to them, so that you can find a way of working together and discussing issues that affect you all. House rules need to be kept by everyone and (if possible) by visitors to your home. It is helpful as far as possible to have the same rules at Granny's, your child minders' and other places your child visits outside the home too.

Rules should be simple with consequences if they are broken. This means that the results of breaking a rule should be thought out in advance with an appropriate sanction agreed. As with any sanction or consequence, this should be for a short duration and repeatable if necessary. Sanctions ideally should be agreed by everyone in advance including the children.

Here are some examples which parents have used as house rules with appropriate sanctions: Swearing or hitting little brother – sanction is that the child loses half an hour of TV time. For jumping on the furniture, the sanction is having to sit quietly for two or three minutes.

Sanctions that are short can easily be repeated and therefore can have more impact than longer ones, when the child with ADHD has forgotten what the sanction was applied for. Remember the sanction should be fair and understandable. You can see above that hitting resulted in a longer and more serious sanction than jumping on the furniture. It is important to make that clear to the child because if he is sent to his room for the same length of time whatever he does, the consequence will not have the same value.

Having established, agreed house rules is a good way of applying rules without appearing to nag. Parents can say 'Oh dear I see you have broken the rule and that means you have to do… Never mind, I am sure you will remember that rule soon'. As your child grows older, you can ask if there is anything you can do to help him remember the rule. This way you are encouraging your child to take responsibility for his behaviour and to see that he can learn, with help, to remember the rules himself. It is good preparation for school when often classroom rules are set out at the beginning of each school year. Even children with ADHD will quickly know the school rules because they are clearly stated and are usually displayed on the wall. Giving the children a visual reminder helps.

It is worth remembering that sanctions alone are not a good method of ensuring your child behaves. There has to be a balance between rewards for good behaviour and sanctions. Praise works much better that sanctions in the long run as it teaches your child how you want him to behave, not how you don't want him to! If possible, move to agreeing positive rules such as we walk slowly, speak to each other respectfully (nicely) and praise your child for keeping these rules. *The better established the rules are at home, the more your child and you will naturally apply them when outside the home.*

📌 Tips on house rules

It is important that you work together on boundaries, limits and rewards. Work with your partner and child to set boundaries and discuss what will happen if these are broken.

Be consistent, fair, but firm, about enforcing sanctions if rules are broken.

Help your child to remember the rules and make sure he understands the consequences of breaking them.

Remind your child if you see that he is about to break a rule, to give him the opportunity to change his own behaviour.

It does not need two parents to enforce a sanction. Both parents individually should be able to enforce a sanction when needed. The parent who is not enforcing the sanction can help the child to act differently next time by saying something like, 'It was a shame Mum had to give you that sanction. I wonder what you could do differently next time to avoid this?' Get the child to come up with ideas. That way he may learn different ways of acting. It is important that you give your child time to calm down before doing this. He needs to be able to come up with ideas with your help.

Remember to use rewards as well as sanctions as much as possible to raise your child's self-esteem.

Skill 7: Rewards

Children generally respond better to rewards than to sanctions and children with ADHD are no different in this respect except that they are often told off for behaviour that is part of their nature. For example they might be

reprimanded for fidgeting, or shouting out rather than putting their hand up in class. These difficulties arise as a result of your child's ADHD characteristics. They are something he can only learn to modify with time and with your support.

Rewards are therefore very important to raise your child's self-esteem about things that he can do well. Rewards should be inexpensive. They can include spending quality time with your child, for example going to the park after school, playing a game together or making up stories. You could give your child tokens to collect. For example when he has five tokens that would equal a trip to the park. If you use tokens make sure you do not take them away once the child has earned them. Apply a different sanction instead. As well as rewarding specific tasks remember to reward when your child is not expecting it and you see him do something well.

Skill 8: Teachable moments in depth

Remember to practice the skills your child is learning outside the home. The good work you are doing with your child at home will help enormously when you are out, and teachable moments not only extend your child's learning, but also show him that the changes you are making in your parenting and communication styles apply as much outside in public as they do back home.

For example counting games can be done walking along the road. Matching the same type of car or lorry can be a good way of making sure your child pays attention. Supermarkets are great learning places as long as you're not doing the weekly shop – choose a time when you are not rushed. Get your child to collect two tins of beans for example that look the same. Or you could take the labels with you and ask your child to find the tins or packets that match what he has on his list. At the checkout see if you can distract him while he waits, and remember to praise him for waiting. Practicing will help your child learn by reinforcement (doing things over and over till he gets the hang of it).

As we have seen, magic carpets can easily be transported to Granny's or the shop if necessary. As we discuss on p. 118, you could keep a square of carpet or a scarf in your bag that could be used as the transportable 'calming down square'.

Tasks for Step 5

Use the checklist at the beginning of this step to see how you are doing. Note the things you find the easiest to do and those you find more difficult. Discuss these with your partner or friend and seek their support if you wish.

Try to find teachable moments in everyday life, so that your use of the skills is transferred across all situations and places. The more you practice the more confident you become and the skills will become second nature to you.

Remember to keep playing with your child for ten minutes each day. Your child will respond to your consistency and over time will learn from this. Behaviour changes in children with ADHD take longer to show, but are very worthwhile.

Parents with symptoms of ADHD themselves

We mentioned at the beginning of the Six-Step Programme that parents with ADHD themselves may have more difficulty than parents without ADHD in carrying out the skills and tasks. We suggest that this is because of their own ADHD symptoms. *If you think your parenting is being affected by your ADHD symptoms, ask someone you trust to help you.* See if they can notice tasks or situations you find difficult and support you in doing these. It is important that you do not choose someone who will take over and direct your behaviour too much as this will only lessen your own self-esteem in managing your child. Pick someone who can help you over time, who understands ADHD, and who you like! A sense of humour may help too.

Remember to keep up using the diaries.

Recap and review

Goal for Step 5

The objective for Step 5 was to review how you are getting on with the skills you have learnt and to transfer these to situations outside of the home.

Skills summary for Step 5

The skills you learned were:

1. listening, sharing feelings and respecting each other
2. expanding the use of timers
3. calming your child
4. using 'earshotting'
5. repeating instructions

6. using house rules outside the home

7. using rewards

8. finding teachable moments.

Tasks summary for Step 5

The tasks you carried out were:

- using the check list to see how you were doing
- playing games for at least ten minutes each day
- keeping diaries for positives and difficult times
- finding teachable moments.

Diary for good days

Date . . . .

Time . . . .

What made it good? . . . .
. . . .
. . . .
. . . .

What did you do? . . . .
. . . .
. . . .
. . . .

Did it help? . . . .
. . . .
. . . .
. . . .
. . . .

How do you feel now? . . . .
. . . .
. . . .
. . . .

Diary for difficult days

Date . . . .

Time . . . .

Trigger . . . .

. . . .

What Happened? . . . .

. . . .

What did you do? . . . .

. . . .

. . . .

Did it help? . . . .

. . . .

. . . .

How do you feel now? . . . .

. . . .

. . . .

Would you do anything different? . . . .

. . . .

. . . .

. . . .

Step **6**

Times Ahead

Goal for Step 6

The aim of the final stage in the programme, is for you to continue to transfer all the skills you have learnt in this manual to everyday situations and to plan how to use them in the future, especially those times around transitions to new stages and places, such as when your child starts or changes school.

Skills overview for Step 6

The two important skills we focus on in this chapter are:

1. how to cope during difficult times
2. how to seek help when you need it.

Tasks overview for Step 6

The tasks you practice in this final step are:

- review the skills learnt in previous steps

- remember to scope and re-assess your child's abilities as he grow older

- remember to look after yourselves

- look at the scenarios in order to review the skills you have attained

- preparing your child for school or going from infants to juniors

- working together with schools.

Introduction to Step 6

This step is about preparing for the future. By now you will have been practicing and gaining confidence in using the skills we have covered and seeing an improvement in how your child responds to you.

We know that children with ADHD have difficulties in times of transition, that is, changing from one situation to another. This could be transitions between parents if you are separated, or changing from infant to junior school for example.

It is important that periods of transition are planned for and your child is prepared for being in different settings. This means working closely together and providing as much consistency as possible between the two places. In order to do this good communication is essential. If you are having difficulties achieving this seek help from professional services early on.

Skill 1: How to cope during difficult times

There are always times in our lives when events challenge us. These include times of bereavement, loss, relationship difficulties or financial difficulty. At these times children pick up on the anxieties of the adults around them. Children's behaviour often appears worse around these times, and children with ADHD are no exception.

This can be for a number of reasons. It may be that you have reduced the amount of time you spend with your child, without realizing it, because of the difficulties. Your child with ADHD may react in several different ways. He might become angry – and this might feel like you are back to how it was before the programme and your interventions. He might demand more attention, and not always in a positive way. If you have had a stressful time and your child's behaviour is worsening when it had been good before, it is worth re-reading the relevant pages of this book again to remind you of what you may have stopped doing. For example sometimes parents relax the house rules unconsciously because of the difficulties they are going through, and this can lead to children acting out to check that the boundaries remain the same. *It is important that you re-establish rules and boundaries as soon as you feel able.* This will help to settle the child's behaviour again.

Children often blame themselves for things that happen. Your child might think, 'Mum and Dad are in a bad mood because I wanted breakfast at the wrong moment,' when parents may have just had a disagreement. Or 'Granny died because I was naughty.' These events are obviously not the child's fault. Reassuring the child and talking about your feelings and his helps your child to understand why times are difficult.

Skill 2: Seeking help when you need it

If the situation is very difficult, and you are struggling to cope, seek support from people you trust. This could be a close friend or relative or a professional. Health visitors, school nurses or your doctor can advise you or point you in the direction of someone willing to and qualified to help. Don't be afraid to ask.

Tasks for Step 6

Reflection on the previous steps and re-assessing your older child

Continue with all the skills you have learned from steps 1-5. We suggest that you continue to work on all of the suggestions from Step 1 through to 5. Eventually the approach will become second nature. The tips that you have learnt work well with all children; you can use them with your other children also. Remember that this programme is for younger children, but the steps can be easily adapted as the child develops. *The same principles remain, you just have to adapt them to the age of your child.*

For example, *quiet time* for teenagers is often in their room, and choices would probably be around clothes or music, for example, 'Do you want this music download or that one?' or '... these trainers or those' 'Do you want to do the dishes now or after Eastenders?'

Helping children and adolescents with their *time perception* would consist of day or weekly planners, getting them to estimate how long tasks take them to complete and then timing themselves to see if they can judge time.

Play and games would be around more sophisticated games such as 'sets' where they have to use visual skills by identifying shapes, colours and patterns. Family games are useful also, as a way of helping your teenager learn to take turns, cope with losing and have fun. For example, Up words, catch phrase, Guess who and so forth.

Looking after yourselves

Children with ADHD can be hard work. The aim of this manual has been to support you in becoming your child's Guide and Trainer, in order to help him overcome some of the difficulties he is experiencing and to help you feel confident in managing his behaviour, knowing that you have the skills to do this.

Even with all the skills you may have been doing already and with what new knowledge you may have acquired, parenting is still hard work. It is important that you *find ways of supporting yourself* in this vital parenting role. Many parents have told us how difficult it is to find time for themselves or indeed time to spend with their partner if they are in a relationship. If you are in any doubt *think about what your child is learning from you as his role model.* Being a role model for your child is not easy, but by showing your child that you need time for you or for you and your partner, you are demonstrating how you maintain your own well-being and relationships with others.

Review the scenarios in this manual

This is the last step of the programme; by now you should have been able to put into practise what you have learnt. It is important to realize that change rarely occurs overnight though and that often it will take a few months to see a significant improvement. *Changing your parenting approach can be difficult*: keep using the guidelines.

Forgive yourself if you cannot practice them all of the time, we are all human. Just try to achieve as much as is possible. We do know from other families that they work.

As already mentioned this book can be used for all children, so if you have other children who are less hyperactive it can help them too. It is, however, specifically aimed at children with ADHD. We have found that for some parents it helps to use the book at least two or three times over a period of few months. You should keep going back through this self-help manual until you are very familiar with all the ideas in it. Some parents will find some ideas easier to work with than others. It can be simple persistence with a particular approach that works in the end, so don't be disheartened if at first things don't appear to change, or if you get times when strategies work less well... Thinking in the long term: this programme can be used with children over longer periods of time if necessary.

Preparing your child for changing school

You might find that the times when your child changes from nursery to school, or from infants to juniors or from junior to senior school, throw up the most difficulties. If so, you may want to go back to study the guidance here again, as at times of developmental change your child may find life difficult and seem to regress. Having to sit still for long periods, coping with school rules, having to wait his turn, doing homework... all these are difficult and challenging skills for the child with ADHD.

You can prepare your child for changes in school. His school will be doing that too. Parents should, if they are happy about doing so, let the child's school know that their child has ADHD and show the child's teacher the Self Help Manual so they can think about whether any of the strategies in it would be helpful to the teaching staff.

Tips on easing school transition

- Help your child to sit still and do colouring or games or look at a book for increasing lengths of time, in preparation for school.
- Get him to practice asking his sister or his friends for toys without snatching.
- Make it clear to your child who will take him to school and pick him up.

Your child will not always remember what you have told him. He may get anxious, and if he is anxious he may appear cross with you or someone else. Sometimes leaving him a reminder note in his lunchbox may help him to recollect what is happening for the rest of the day. Notes of encouragement will help him feel reassured during the day.

To conclude: general hints and tips

Children with ADHD are hard to parent; they call on all your parenting skills. Continue to work with your partner to be consistent with the messages you present to your child.

Go back to the beginning of the book if you need to remind yourself what to do. Use the checklists to see if you are maintaining use of the skills. *Be kind to yourself.* Seek the support of others to let off steam too. Make sure you have time to yourself and with your partner. It is a good example to set, as well as essential to maintain your relationship.

Forgive yourself if you have a bad day – we all do sometimes. Enlist the support of others. Family and friends can be lifesavers when the going gets tough.

We have included some scenarios for you to practice the skills you've acquired and you can review how your interactions are going. You will find these in the workbook section at the back of the manual (pp. 154–157)

We have put in another copy of the parents' checklist for you to remind yourself how you are doing, and to remind you to check up on tasks you may need to go back and revise on p. 159. The numbers for the skills, the table of contents and the index should help you locate the areas of the book you want to return to.

Remember your child's symptoms should become easier for you and him to control as time goes on with the programme, but school might be a challenge (which can be positive as well as negative).

Note about Medication

This manual has not given information about medication which may be used successfully to help treat the symptoms of ADHD. Further information would be available from your primary care doctor, clinic doctor or nurse. You may well not need further help but if you do try to see professionals in a favourable light. They can help.

Sometimes the strategies in this manual may not have been enough to control your child's symptoms, especially at school. If this is the case then medication might help. If children do need medication, research tells us that if it is used by parents who use the strategies in this manual, their children will need smaller doses and therefore have fewer side-effects from the medication.

By reading this book and adopting the strategies suggested you are well on the way to improving things for you, your child and your family. Congratulations and very best wishes for the future.

Diary for good days

Date . . . .

Time . . . .

What made it good? . . . .

. . . .

. . . .

. . . .

What did you do? . . . .

. . . .

. . . .

. . . .

Did it help? . . . .

. . . .

. . . .

. . . .

. . . .

How do you feel now? . . . .

. . . .

. . . .

. . . .

Diary for difficult days

Date . . . .

Time . . . .

Trigger . . . .
. . . .

What Happened? . . . .
. . . .
. . . .

What did you do? . . . .
. . . .
. . . .

Did it help? . . . .
. . . .
. . . .

How do you feel now? . . . .
. . . .
. . . .

Would you do anything different? . . . .
. . . .
. . . .

Resources

Practise Scenarios

The scenarios below are fictional but draw on our extensive experience of working with children with ADHD and their parents. You should treat them as multiple choice quizzes.

Tom is always having problems playing; his concentration is poor lasting only a few minutes. What can you do?

1. Tell him he has to sit down and play.

2. Ignore this, he will learn one day.

3. Help him by setting regular time aside to play with him to enable him to practise.

    Clue: Children with ADHD often miss vital steps in how to play.

You sent Rachael upstairs to get her school bag. She hasn't returned downstairs and she will be late for school. Do you:

1. Remind Rachael what she went for and give her a time limit to come downstairs with it?

2. Shout at Rachael; tell her she will be late?

3. Go upstairs and get the bag yourself?

   Clue: Children with ADHD have short-term memory problems.

Jimmy comes out of school and runs about dangerously all the way home. Do you:

1. Pick him up in the car?

2. Put him on reins to ensure he is embarrassed in front of his friends and will stop the running about?

3. Understand that he probably needs to be active after a day concentrating; arrange a deal that if he walks next to you he can go to the park on the way home?

   Clue: ADHD children find it hard to concentrate all day; they need to let off steam.

Bradley's teacher meets you when you pick him up asking to have a word about his difficult behaviour, you talk to her. Do you:

1. Feel embarrassed, tell Bradley off on the way home – ask him why he is so naughty?

2. Wait until you get home, talk to Bradley about his day, what was good and what wasn't, and give him ideas to prevent it happening again.

3. Punish him when you get home – it is important to make sure he knows he will be punished if he is naughty again.

   Clue: Children with ADHD find it hard to problem solve. By exploring difficulties freely you can help them learn to act differently.

Bradley is still having difficulties in school; the teacher calls you in for the third time that week. Do you:

1.   Go in and speak to him, feel embarrassed and helpless and go home?

2.   Do you ask a friend/partner to join you, arrange a further regular time to meet and ask the teacher what support is being arranged for Bradley and himself in school?

3.   Stop picking him up from school, send a friend?

> *Clue: It is important that you obtain as much support for your child and possible and that people coming into contact with him understand his difficulties.*

You tell Amy off. She shouts and says you don't love her. Do you:

•   Tell her you don't love her?

•   Get upset, plead with her that you do?

•   Say to her that you think she is upset that you have told her off, that you do love her but that she has to stop what she is doing.

> *Clue: Be strong. Separate the behaviour from the child, whilst being consistent.*

Review Sheet

Use the review sheet below according to the instructions on p. 83 and 102. It is a very helpful tool for assessing your child's abilities. Make more of your own if you run out of space.

Review Sheet

Date	What are you observing?	How long did it take your child to complete this task?	Did your child manage these?	Did he require help?

Parents' Checklist for Self-monitoring

Here is a short questionnaire based on the ideas in the Six Step Parenting Programme. We hope by completing this you can see how you are doing in using the tasks and skills we have introduced in the programme. Are there some you find easier to do than others? Sometimes we avoid doing what we find most difficult. Or we have just forgotten to do some tasks. The questionnaire is a way for you to check for yourself, and assess which strategies you are using well, and what needs further practise. It is sometimes helpful to complete this with your partner as you will each have things that you find easier to do and you may be able to support one another with aspects of the programme you find difficult.

Parents checklist for self-monitoring

		Not at all	A little	Often
1	I remember to get my child's attention before giving instructions			
2	I remember to use eye contact for positives			
3	I am good at giving praise frequently			
4	My partner and I work closely together to manage our child			
5	I am consistent			
6	I give clear messages to my child			
7	I use countdowns when my child needs to change from what he's doing			
8	I have clear behaviour boundaries			
9	I avoid rows and keep calm, I anticipate difficult times			
10	I practice giving my child limited choices			
11	I use the word 'we' rather than 'you'			
12	I play games with my child to improve his attention for at least ten minutes each day			
13	I have practiced using quiet time with my child			
14	I make sure I speak with the appropriate voice to my child			
15	I talk about how I feel and encourage my child to do the same			
16	I listen to what my child is saying to me			
17	I try to expand his play by describing what he is doing			
18	I manage any outbursts well			
19	I manage to anticipate and distract my child preventing outbursts			
20	I use timers often			
21	I praise my child's behaviour to others (Granny etc)			
22	I remember to repeat instructions to my child			
23	I have clearly displayed house rules			
24	I regularly review my child's ability in order to help him progress			
25	I regularly reflect on how I am doing as a parent			

Further Information about ADHD

The following books and websites offer information and support for parents and children with a diagnosis of ADHD.

Books

Serfontein, G. (2005) *The Hidden Handicap: How to help children who suffer from Dyslexia, Hyperactivity and Learning Difficulties.* Australia: Simon and Schuster.

Green, C. and Chee, K. (1995) *Understanding Attention Deficit Disorder.* New York: Vermillion.

Zelgler Dendy, Chris A. (1990) *Teenagers with ADHD/ADD: A Parents Guide.* Fawcett Columbine: Woodbine House Inc.

Websites

Attention Deficit Disorder Association – www.add.org

ADDISS (ADHD information Service) – www.addiss.co.uk/

CHADD (Children and Adults with Attention Deficit Hyperactivity Disorder) – www.chadd.org

Young Minds – www.youngminds.org.uk

Mental Health Foundation – www.mentalhealth.org.uk

Royal College of Psychiatrists – www.rcpsych.ac.uk
Index locators marked in italics, identifies information presented in tables or diagrams.

Index